CAMBRIDGE PRIMARY
Global Perspectives

Learner's Skills Book 5

Adrian Ravenscroft & Thomas Holman

Shaftesbury Road, Cambridge CB2 8EA, United Kingdom

One Liberty Plaza, 20th Floor, New York, NY 10006, USA

477 Williamstown Road, Port Melbourne, VIC 3207, Australia

314–321, 3rd Floor, Plot 3, Splendor Forum, Jasola District Centre, New Delhi – 110025, India

103 Penang Road, #05–06/07, Visioncrest Commercial, Singapore 238467

Cambridge University Press is part of the University of Cambridge.

It furthers the University's mission by disseminating knowledge in the pursuit of education, learning and research at the highest international levels of excellence.

www.cambridge.org
Information on this title: www.cambridge.org/9781009325707

First published 2021
Second edition 2024

20 19 18 17 16 15 14 13 12 11 10 9 8 7 6 5 4 3 2

Printed in Poland by Opolgraf

A catalogue record for this publication is available from the British Library

ISBN 978-1-009-32570-7 Learner's Skills Book 5 with Digital Access (1 Year)

CAMBRIDGE DEDICATED TEACHER AWARDS 2023

Teachers play an important part in shaping futures.
Our Dedicated Teacher Awards recognise the hard work that teachers put in every day.

Thank you to everyone who nominated this year; we have been inspired and moved by all of your stories. Well done to all of our nominees for your dedication to learning and for inspiring the next generation of thinkers, leaders and innovators.

CONGRATULATIONS TO OUR INCREDIBLE WINNERS!

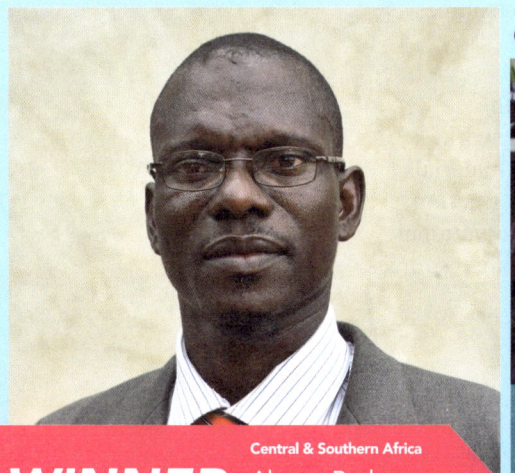

WINNER
Central & Southern Africa
Akeem Badru
St Michael R.C.M Primary School, Ogunpa Lunloye, Nigeria

Regional Winner: East & South Asia
Gaurav Sharma
FirstSteps School, India

Regional Winner: North & South America
Nathalie Roy
Glasgow Middle School, United States

Regional Winner: Australia, New Zealand & South-East Asia
Goh Kok Ming
SJKC Hua Lian 1, Malaysia

Regional Winner: Middle East & North Africa
Uzma Siraj
Future World School, Pakistan

Regional Winner: Europe
Selçuk Yusuf Arslan
Atatürk MTAL, Turkey

For more information about our dedicated teachers and their stories, go to **dedicatedteacher.cambridge.org**

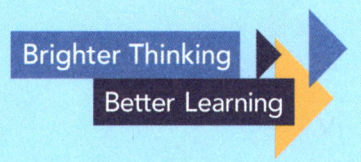

Endorsement statement

Endorsement indicates that a resource has passed Cambridge International's rigorous quality-assurance process and is suitable to support the delivery of a Cambridge International curriculum framework. However, endorsed resources are not the only suitable materials available to support teaching and learning, and are not essential to be used to achieve the qualification. Resource lists found on the Cambridge International website will include this resource and other endorsed resources.

Any example answers to questions taken from past question papers, practice questions, accompanying marks and mark schemes included in this resource have been written by the authors and are for guidance only. They do not replicate examination papers. In examinations the way marks are awarded may be different. Any references to assessment and/or assessment preparation are the publisher's interpretation of the curriculum framework requirements. Examiners will not use endorsed resources as a source of material for any assessment set by Cambridge International.

While the publishers have made every attempt to ensure that advice on the qualification and its assessment is accurate, the official curriculum framework, specimen assessment materials and any associated assessment guidance materials produced by the awarding body are the only authoritative source of information and should always be referred to for definitive guidance. Cambridge International recommends that teachers consider using a range of teaching and learning resources based on their own professional judgement of their students' needs.

Cambridge International has not paid for the production of this resource, nor does Cambridge International receive any royalties from its sale. For more information about the endorsement process, please visit www.cambridgeinternational.org/endorsed-resources

Cambridge International copyright material in this publication is reproduced under licence and remains the intellectual property of Cambridge Assessment International Education.

Contents

Contents

Introduction

Cambridge Global Perspectives™ is all about helping you to develop a set of important skills.

Throughout the book, four characters – Zara, Sofia, Arun and Marcus – will be with you every step of the way. They will be asking useful questions and sharing their own ideas about some issues that they are exploring. You will see that word 'issue' a lot in this book. In Cambridge Global Perspectives, an issue is an important subject or problem for discussion.

The skills you learn will be useful in the other subjects you are studying now, but also in your future studies, and in your life beyond school. The six key skills you will be learning are:

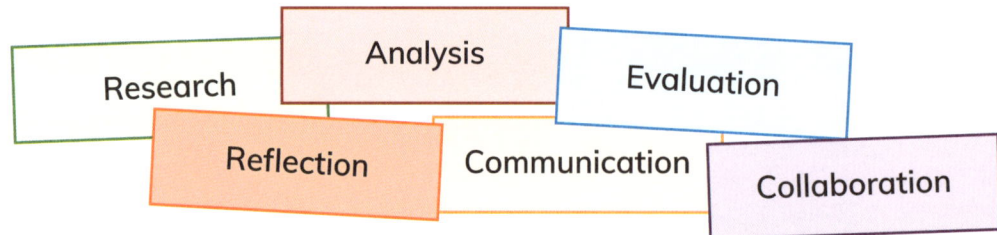

You don't need to know any facts to start off with. Each of the six chapters in this book focuses on a different one of these skills and is full of fun activities to help you improve. At the end of each of the chapters, you will have a chance to reflect on all the different ways that you have used the focus skill and improved your understanding.

While developing these skills, you will also learn about some interesting topics, including 'Health and wellbeing', 'Education for all', and 'Looking after planet Earth', and think about important issues within these topics. A few of the questions you will find in this book are 'WhHow can we stay healthy?', 'Where does all our packaging go?' and 'What prevents some children from getting a primary school education?' You will find out about different perspectives on these issues and you will also need to think about what actions you could take in your school or your local area to have a positive impact on some of these issues.

Because each chapter focuses on a different skill, you don't need to work through the book from beginning to end, one chapter at a time. Depending on what else your class is learning about, your teacher might want you to focus on different skills at different times, or to work across different chapters. Each chapter follows the same order, going from 'Starting with' to 'Developing' and finally 'Getting better at', so that you can build up your confidence in each skill.

Sometimes you will be exploring the same issue as Zara, Marcus, Arun and Sofia. At other times, your teacher may want you to use the same skills to explore a similar issue focusing on what is important to people in your school, or your local area.

Your teacher will provide you with additional material and other useful resources to help you complete the activities in the book. There are also three projects that your teacher may ask you to complete, to showcase the skills you have gained!

How to use this book

This book contains lots of different features that will help your learning. These are explained below.

You can use these learning goals to identify what you are learning in the lesson, and how you know when you have met your goals.

Lesson learning goals

These are the goals for this lesson.
You will return to this table at the end of the lesson for the independent reflection activity.

My learning goals To start to:	I think	My teacher/ partner thinks
identify different types of question		
make my own questions to help me understand an issue		

These are questions or tasks to help check what you already know before beginning a lesson.

What can I already do?

Two of Zara's neighbours are having an disagreement:

- Neighbour A complains that Neighbour B plays loud music late at night.
- Neighbour B's window has been broken, and Neighbour B believes that Neighbour A's children are responsible because they like playing football outside.

Talk with a partner. What do you think the two neighbours should do in order to resolve their disagreement? What changes could each neighbour make?

This is a chance for you to record the issue that you will be thinking about in each lesson. Sometimes this will be the same issue the characters are working on; sometimes your teacher might want you to use the skills you learn as part of a project focused on your school or your local area.

The issue I am focusing on today is:

....

New and important words are orange in the text. You can find out what they mean in the glossary at the back of the book.

Marcus has been thinking about what different park users need in order to enjoy their visit. He uses a Venn diagram to show what each group needs. Complete the diagram. One example has been done for you.

This helps you check how you are learning, and think about how well you are progressing with each goal at the end of each lesson. ────────▶

Independent reflection activity

Check your learning goals

If you have achieved them and could teach someone else, put a '★'.

If you have achieved them independently, put a '☺'.

If you can achieve them with support, put a '☺'.

This allows you to consider your progress through the learning goals in a deeper way. The table encourages you to think about where you are on your learning journey. You can choose goals to improve on in the future. ────────▶

Self-assessment Lesson 5

How will I know if I have achieved my learning goals?

Use this activity to reflect on how well you have progressed over the last lesson.

Tick (✓) 'Achieved independently' if you feel confident that you could apply this skill for yourself.

Tick (✓) 'Achieved with support' if you still need some help when you apply this skill.

If you tick 'Achieved independently', then try to deepen your understanding and provide support for others when working on the next issue.

If you tick 'Achieved with support', look out for opportunities to consolidate this skill when working on the next issue.

Evaluation learning goals To get better at:	Achieved independently	Achieved with support	I think this because
discussing a source, its author and purpose and its strengths and limitations			
saying what I think about someone else's perspective			

This provides an opportunity to reflect on your focus issue as you progress through each skill. ────────▶

Issue review

Think about the issue you have been focusing on and complete the following statements.

I was surprised to discover/explore that ....

....

I did not know ....

....

I now think ....

....

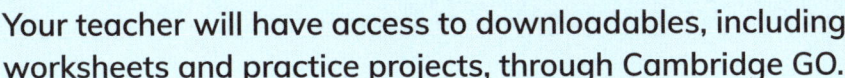

Your teacher will have access to downloadables, including worksheets and practice projects, through Cambridge GO.

Acknowledgements

The authors and publishers acknowledge the following sources of copyright material and are grateful for the permissions granted. While every effort has been made, it has not always been possible to identify the sources of all the material used, or to trace all copyright holders. If any omissions are brought to our notice, we will be happy to include the appropriate acknowledgements on reprinting.

Thanks to the following for permission to reproduce images:

Cover Pablo Gallego/Beehive Illustration

Inside **Unit 1** Lucas Ninno/GI; Danishkhan/GI; Roberto Westbrook/GI; Westend61/GI; Itsskin/GI; Irina Vodneva/GI; Manolo Guijarro/GI; Rosley Majid/GI; Bartosz Hadyniak/GI; Nick David/GI; Pictures Ltd/GI; Nitat Termmee/GI; Monkeybusinessimages/GI; Sam Panthaky/GI; Riccardo Lennart Niels Mayer/GI; Stockplanets/GI; Amorn Suriyan/GI; Recep-Bg/GI; Masterzphotois/GI; Ariel Skelley/GI (X2); Aapsky/GI; Mayur Kakade/GI; Anantagarwal/GI; Solstock/GI; Pakin Songmor/GI; **Unit 2** Jose Luis Pelaez Inc/GI; Thianchai Sitthikongsak/GI; Marko Geber/GI; Digital Vision/GI; FG Trade Latin/GI; Shih-Wei/GI; Matteo Colombo/GI; Jittawit.21/GI; Jackf/GI; Halfpoint/GI; Timsa/GI; Yusufozluk/GI; Brianajackson/GI; Frans Lemmens/GI; Toniflap/GI; Tim Graham/GI; Vichie81/GI; Morsa Images/GI (X4); Haykirdi/GI (X2); Vladimir Godnik/GI (X2); Devid75/GI; Jeffrey Greenberg/GI; Mike Kemp/In Picture/GI; Thomas Barwick/GI; Images By Tang Ming Tung/GI; SolStock/GI; Rudimencial/GI; Kinzie Riehm/GI; **Unit 3** Carol Yepes/GI; Richvintage/GI; Tim Platt/GI; Johner Images/GI; Cultura RM Exclusive/Flynn Larsen/GI; Zdravinjo/GI; Dies-Irae/GI; FG Trade/GI; Byrdyak/GI; Monkeybusinessimages/GI; **Unit 4** Andersen Ross Photography Inc/GI; Ariel Skelley/GI; Westend61/GI; Flashpop/GI; FG Trade/GI; Insta_Photos/GI; Jonathan Kirn/GI; SDI Productions/GI; Narisara Nami/GI; Images By Tang Ming Tung/GI; Kali9/GI; Emmanuel Lavigne/GI; Leon Neal/GI; Yuichiro Chino/GI; Bartosz Hadyniak/GI; Carol Yepes/GI; Mclninch/GI; FG Trade/GI; Westend61/GI; Anastasiia Boriagina/GI; Camille Tokerud/GI; SDI Productions/GI; Dglimages/GI; Dinodia Photo/GI; Hadynyah/GI; Christophe Boisvieux/GI; Greenaperture/GI; Vgajic/GI; Jonas Gratzer/GI; FatCamera/GI; Jupiterimages/GI; Hill Street Studios/GI; Khalus/GI; **Unit 5** Matthias Tunger/GI; Mayur Kakade/GI; Stephen Barnes/GI; Nurphoto/GI; Paul Hauf/GI; Vedfelt/GI; Howard Grey/GI; Thomas Barwick/GI; FatCamera/GI; **Unit 6** Ariel Skelley/GI; Caia Image/GI; Kali9/GI; Comstock/GI; Imgorthand/GI; Solstock/GI; Cavan Images/GI; Tevarak Phanduang/GI; Fatcamera/GI; Jose Luis Pelaez Inc/GI

Key: GI= Getty Images.

> Section 1

Research

In this section of your Learner's Skills Book you'll be developing your research skills while thinking about interesting global issues.

But what does research involve?

Let's start thinking about research!

In Section 1: Research, you might choose to focus on the Challenge 'How much water do we use?' and the topic 'Water, food and farming'.

If you take on this Challenge, you and your group may carry out research to find out how much water is needed to make and use some common products. An example could be a t-shirt made of cotton. Here are some of the questions you could ask as you carry out your research:

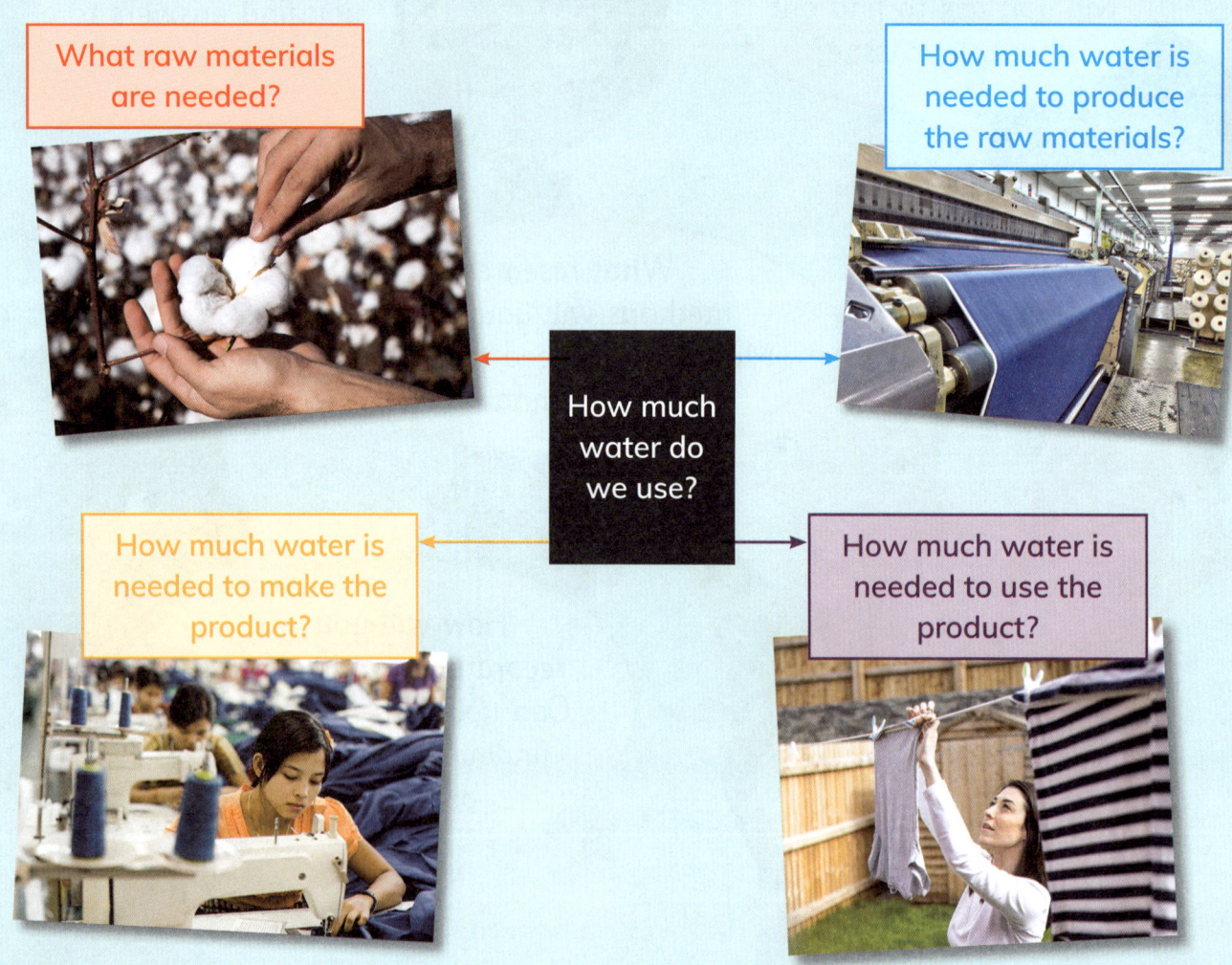

What raw materials are needed?

How much water is needed to produce the raw materials?

How much water do we use?

How much water is needed to make the product?

How much water is needed to use the product?

Other things to think about:

- What sources can we use?
- What are our predictions?
- What method can we use?
- How can we record what we find out?

Or you might choose to focus on the topics 'Health and wellbeing' and 'Looking after planet Earth', which you will look at in this section of your Learner's Skills Book.

Think about your answers to these questions:

- What questions can I ask to find out about an issue?
- What do I think the answers will be?
- What sources can I use?
- What methods can I use?
- How can I record information clearly?

Research words

answer	graph	investigation	prediction	record
chart	information	method	question	source
findings	interview	notes	questionnaire	survey

What is research?

Research: asking questions to find out about an issue

Research also includes:

- deciding what sources to use
- making predictions
- choosing a method to carry out research
- recording information

Remember!

You can use any of the Challenges or topics as the starting point to develop your research skills. Your teacher may direct you to focus on a specific Challenge or topic, or you may be able to choose for yourself.

Starting with research skills: Lesson 1

In this chapter you will develop skills in **research**. In general, research means investigating an **issue** or **topic** in order to get **information** about it. In Cambridge Primary Global Perspectives, research may involve making **questions** or **predictions** to help you find out more about an issue, finding **sources** that contain useful information, carrying out **investigations** using **interviews** and/or **questionnaires**, and presenting the results of an investigation.

Lesson learning goals

These are the goals for this lesson.
You will return to this table at the end of the lesson for the independent reflection activity.

My learning goals To start to:	I think	My teacher/ partner thinks
identify different types of question		
make my own questions to help me understand an issue		

What can I already do?

Choice 1: water

What comes to mind when you think of 'how I use water'?

Compare your list with a partner's. What similarities and differences are there?

Have a class discussion – how can we categorise the different ways we use water?

Choice 2: our own issue

What comes to mind when you think of 'how I use .... '?

Compare your list with a partner's. What similarities and differences are there?

Have a class discussion – how can we categorise the different ways we use things?

Starter activity

The issue I am focusing on today is:

....

Marcus is thinking of how water is used in his home area, and also some problems that water can cause.

Issue	Water usage	
Positive uses	• Drinking it – especially on a hot day • Watering the plants • Cleaning the house • Washing ourselves • Washing the car • Washing our bikes • Filling the canal	• Cleaning our teeth • Cooking • Swimming pool • In the factory, the workers cool metal – it makes a lot of steam! • Keeping the cricket pitch healthy and green
Problems caused	• When it rains a lot, the drains overflow and the bottom of the road gets flooded. • Cars can't get past.	• We can't play football on the grass when it is too muddy. • When I was in Stage 2, the river flooded and people down the road had to move out.

Now think about *either* water in your home area or something connected to an issue that you are focusing on. You can discuss these with your partner.

Write down how it is used and some problems it can cause.

Issue		
Positive uses		
Problems caused		

Main activity part 1

Zara is thinking of questions that she could use to help her find out more about the issue she is focusing on.

She has thought of many questions. Read her thoughts below:

What do we use water for in our school?

Who supplies the school's water?

?

When does it rain too much so that the river floods?

How did they make the bridge better?

Class discussion

1   What other questions could Zara add to her mind map?

or

2   What questions could you ask about the issue you are investigating?

Main activity part 2

Zara's group has thought of some good questions.

- Some are about how water is used.
- Some are about how water can cause problems.

Which is which? Discuss with a partner and fill in the table below.
Two have been done for you.

	Using water	Problems caused by water
What do we use water for in our school?	✓	
Who supplies the school's water?		
Where does the water in our school come from?		
When does it rain too much so that the river floods?		✓
Why did it flood at the bottom of the road?		
How did they make the bridge better?		

With your group, think of questions that focus on the issue of how we can use water more sustainably – or on another issue that you are investigating.

Check you have thought of a good range of questions:

- some about uses
- some about problems.

Use the download that your teacher will give you to write your questions.
Tick (✓) whether the question is about uses or about problems.

Share your ideas with others in the class.

Independent reflection activity

Check your learning goals

If you have achieved them and could teach someone else, put a '★'.

If you have achieved them independently, put a '☺'.

If you can achieve them with support, put a '☺'.

Starting with research skills: Lesson 2

Lesson learning goals

These are the goals for this lesson.
You will return to this table at the end of the lesson for the independent reflection activity.

| My learning goals
To start to: | I think | My teacher/
partner thinks |
|---|---|---|
| recognise different sources that can help me to find out about an issue | | |
| design a questionnaire to use in an investigation | | |
| make simple predictions about what I think I will find out in an investigation | | |

What can I already do?

Sofia has been thinking of questions about the issue of using water sustainably in her area.

1   Who uses the most water in our class? i. Ask some parents ....

2   What do they use to clean our water? ....

3   How do we waste water in our school? ....

4   Where can we find water locally? ....

5   Where does our tap water come from? ....

6   When does it rain most in our area? ....

7   Why did it flood at the bottom of the road? ....

Arun has been collecting some possible sources of information.

a   The website of the local newspaper   f   A map of the city

b   An atlas of the country   g   The website of the local water board

c   A world atlas   h   A questionnaire to ask students

d   Ask school staff   i   Ask some parents

e   A dictionary

Can you help Sofia and Arun match the questions to the sources that would give them answers?

Tips: you might need some more than once. Some might not be so useful.
The first one has been done for you.

Starter activity

The issue I am focusing on today is:

....

Work in pairs.

One person should make a list of questions about your issue.
One person should make a list of sources of information.
Then get together to match the questions to the sources.

Questions	Sources of information

Main activity part 1

Sofia and Arun have thought of
a question that they could answer
by asking the children in their class.

How often do we
use water in our
class?

They have designed a questionnaire to help them gather information.
Study their questionnaire below.

How often do we (or does someone in your house) ...?	Several times a day	Once a day	Several times a week	Once a week	Less often
Brush their teeth					
Make tea					
Make coffee					
Put the washing machine on					
Water the garden					
Wash the car					
Wash the dishes					
Take a bath					
Take a shower					

What do you predict the results of Sofia and Arun's questionnaire might show?

....

Class discussion

Share your thoughts in a class discussion.

Main activity part 2

The issue I am focusing on today is:

....

In your group, decide on a question you could answer by asking the children in your class.

How often do we .... in our class?

Use the download that your teacher will give you to design a questionnaire to help you gather information.

Sofia and Arun have been thinking about what their results might show:

In my house, they're always drinking tea. I think most people in the class will be the same.

My uncle's taxi is always clean. I predict most children will say they clean the car every day.

Discuss with your group what you think you might find. Give **reasons** for your answer.

Independent reflection activity

Check your learning goals

If you have achieved them and could teach someone else, put a '★'.

If you have achieved them independently, put a '☺'.

If you can achieve them with support, put a '☺'.

3

Starting with research skills: Lesson 3

Lesson learning goals		
These are the goals for this lesson. You will return to this table at the end of the lesson for the independent reflection activity.		
My learning goals To start to:	I think	My teacher/ partner thinks
find information in sources to answer my own questions		
think of my own questions to ask when interviewing someone		
recognise different ways of selecting, organising and recording information from sources		

What can I already do?

Sofia and her group are planning an investigation. They thought of some steps they should take. What steps do you think have been missed out from their table?

Step number	Action
1	Decide on an issue we can investigate.
2	
3	
4	
5	
6	Tell others what we found out.

Starter activity

Sofia and Arun have been using their questionnaire to ask others in their class about their water use.

Marcus says: 'Everybody in my family brushes their teeth twice a day. My dad makes tea all the time. My mum drinks coffee once a day, but no one else likes it. We put the washing machine on several times a week. We water the garden every day in the summer. To be honest, we might not wash the car that much – maybe once a month. We wash the dishes several times a day. My sister takes a bath once a week, but the rest of us take showers.'

1   Is there any information they can record on their table based on what Marcus has said?

2   Are there any additional questions they might need to ask before they can fill in the table?

How often do we (or does someone in your house) ...?	Several times a day	Once a day	Several times a week	Once a week	Less often
Brush their teeth					
Make tea					
Make coffee					
Put the washing machine on					
Water the garden					
Wash the car					
Wash the dishes					
Take a bath					
Take a shower					

Main activity

The issue I am focusing on today is:

....

Class discussion

1 What difficulties might you come across when you ask people questions for your survey?

2 How can you overcome these?

Use the questionnaire that you designed in Lesson 2 to find out about your issue from other members in your class.

15 >

Peer feedback

When you have finished your survey, find someone who answered your questions and ask them to tell you:

Two things that they like about your questions in the survey (write what they tell you here):

⭐ ....

⭐ ....

One thing that you could do better (write what they tell you here):

 ....

Independent reflection activity

Check your learning goals

If you have achieved them and could teach someone else, put a '★'.

If you have achieved them independently, put a '☺'.

If you can achieve them with support, put a '☺'.

Self-assessment Lessons 1–3

How will I know if I have achieved my learning goals?

Use this activity to reflect on how well you have progressed over the last three lessons.

Tick (✓) 'Achieved independently' if you feel confident that you could apply this skill for yourself.

Tick (✓) 'Achieved with support' if you still need some help when you apply this skill.

If you tick 'Achieved independently', then try to deepen your understanding and provide support for others when working on the next issue.

If you tick 'Achieved with support', look out for opportunities to consolidate this skill when working on the next issue.

Continued

Research learning goals To start to:	Achieved independently	Achieved with support	I think this because
identify different types of question about an issue and make my own questions to help me understand more about it			
recognise different sources of information and find information in them to answer my questions			
use answers to my questions and find information in other sources to help me understand more about an issue			
make simple predictions about what I think I will find out in an investigation			
recognise different ways of selecting, organising and recording information from sources			

Issue review

Think about the issue you have been focusing on and complete the following statements.

I was surprised to discover/explore that ....

....

I did not know ....

....

I now think ....

....

Developing research skills: Lesson 4

Lesson learning goals		
These are the goals for this lesson. You will return to this table at the end of the lesson for the independent reflection activity.		
My learning goals To develop my knowledge and understanding about:	I think	My teacher/ partner thinks
making questions that can help me investigate an issue		

What can I already do?

Sofia's class recently went on a school trip to a museum. After the visit, Sofia was asked to get some feedback from her classmates. Which of these questions would help the school to find out if the trip had been a success? Put them in order from 1 (most helpful question) to 6 (least helpful question).

a   Did you enjoy your visit to the museum? ☐

b   What did you like most about your visit to the museum? ☐

c   When did you visit the museum? ☐

d   Was it your first visit to the museum? ☐

e   What did you learn from your visit to the museum? ☐

f   Would you like to make another visit to the museum? ☐

Talk to a partner. Tell them which question you thought was the most helpful question and why.

What other helpful questions could Sofia ask?

Starter activity

The issue I am focusing on today is:

....

Marcus is very lucky as he lives in an area where tap water is safe to drink. He and his family drink mainly tap water, but he has seen a lot of his classmates drinking bottled water. This is water that is sold mainly in plastic bottles with a brand name on the bottle. Marcus thinks of some of the pros and cons of drinking bottled water, and starts making a list.

Complete the list with your own ideas, and then share your thoughts with the group.

Bottled water

Pros	Cons
• Taste	•
•	•
•	•
•	•
•	•

Class discussion

1 Do you prefer to drink bottled water or tap water? Why?
2 What other reasons could there be for drinking bottled water or tap water?
3 How could you investigate the issue of why people choose to drink bottled water?

Main activity part 1

Marcus wants to change people's behaviour, so that they drink less bottled water. First of all, he needs to understand the choices that his classmates make.

Which of these questions do you think will help him the most to understand his classmates' behaviour?

a Who decides what you drink every day?
b Do you prefer drinking bottled water or tap water?
c What is the main reason you drink bottled water?
d How much bottled water do you drink every day?
e What is your favourite drink?

Be ready to share your thoughts with the class.

Class discussion

1 Which question would be the best question for Marcus to investigate? Why?

2 What other questions could he investigate in order to change his classmates' behaviour?

3 What step in his investigation do you think Marcus should take next?

Main activity part 2

Marcus decides that he will ask his classmates the question 'What is the main reason you drink bottled water?'

1 What would your answer be to this question?

....

2 What other answers do you think there will be to Marcus's question?

....

....

3 How could you find out the most popular answer to Marcus's question?

....

....

Share your ideas with others in the class.

Independent reflection activity

Check your learning goals

If you have achieved them and could teach someone else, put a '★'.

If you have achieved them independently, put a '☺'.

If you can achieve them with support, put a '☺'.

5

Developing research skills: Lesson 5

What can I already do?

Marcus understands that note-taking is a quick way of recording information from a source.

In a source about bottled water, Marcus reads:

> Bottled water is the most popular drink in the world. It is estimated that, on average, everyone consumes approximately 50 litres of bottled water every year.

These are the notes Marcus takes:

BW = world's most popular drink

1 person drinks approx. 50 l BW per yr

Marcus used the following note-taking techniques to make his notes quick and efficient. Give an example of each from his notes.

	Example
abbreviations	
symbols	
shorter words / phrases	

Talk with a partner. Which of these techniques do you use when you take notes?
What other examples of each technique can you think of?
What other techniques of note-taking do you use?

Starter activity

The issue I am focusing on today is:

....

Marcus thinks that drinking bottled water may not be sustainable. These are some of the questions that he and his group would like to find the answers to:

Look at the questions for the class discussion below.
Talk to a partner and prepare some answers to share with the class.

Class discussion

1   What do you think the answers to these questions might be?
2   Where could you find the answers to these questions?
3   How could you record the answers?

Main activity part 1

Work in a group. In your group, decide who will answer each of the questions Marcus and his team ask in the Starter activity. Write your question here:

My question:

....

Your teacher will give you a source to read. On a separate piece of paper, note down any information in the source that answers your question.

Peer feedback

Work with a partner from your group.
Show them your notes and ask them to decide if these statements are true:

- The notes only contain information about the question.   Yes/No
- The notes record the information in a quick and efficient way.   Yes/No

Ask your partner to tell you one way that you could improve your notes.

....

Main activity part 2

Now share the information in your notes with the others in your group.
Listen to what the others in your group tell you.
Note down three more pieces of information about bottled water:

1 ....

2 ....

3 ....

Class discussion

1 What is the most important piece of information you have learned about bottled water? Why?

2 What could Marcus do to persuade people in his area to drink less bottled water?

Independent reflection activity

Check your learning goals

If you have achieved them and could teach someone else, put a '★'.

If you have achieved them independently, put a '☺'.

If you can achieve them with support, put a '☺'.

Developing research skills: Lesson 6

Lesson learning goals

These are the goals for this lesson.
You will return to this table at the end of the lesson for the independent reflection activity.

My learning goals To develop my knowledge and understanding about:	I think	My teacher/ partner thinks
thinking of my own questions to ask when interviewing someone		
designing my own questionnaire to use in an investigation		

What can I already do?

Marcus talks to some of his classmates. Some drink bottled water; others prefer to drink tap water. Marcus notes down what they say. Tick (✓) the statements that could be given as a reason for drinking bottled water. One example has been done for you.

Statements		
1 'It's too expensive.'	2 'The plastic can be recycled.' ✓	3 'I prefer the taste.'
4 'It's cool! I love the advertisements.'	5 'It creates litter and causes pollution.'	6 'It's healthier than drinking sugary drinks.'
7 'It's healthier and safer.'	8 'It doesn't come from local sources.'	9 'I think all water tastes the same.'
10 'You can boil or filter water to make it safe.'	11 'I can take it with me wherever I go.'	12 'We use too much plastic.'

Talk with a partner. Find out if your partner prefers drinking bottled water or tap water.

Which of these statements does your partner agree with?

Starter activity

The issue I am focusing on today is:

....

Marcus wants to find out why people choose to drink bottled water instead of tap water. He discusses with his group the reasons that he thinks people will give him. Read what Marcus and his group say, and think about your own answers to the questions for the discussion that follows.

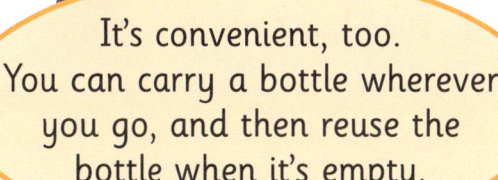

I think most people will say that they prefer the taste of bottled water to tap water.

Some people will say that it's cheaper than buying other sorts of drink, and healthier than drinking sugary drinks.

Others might believe the advertisements that say bottled water is healthier and safer than tap water.

It's convenient, too. You can carry a bottle wherever you go, and then reuse the bottle when it's empty.

Class discussion

1   How could Marcus investigate the reasons his classmates choose to drink bottled water?
2   How could he record the results of his investigation?

Main activity

Marcus decides to ask his classmates to rank (put in order of importance) their reasons for choosing to drink bottled water. He designs this questionnaire:

Reasons for drinking bottled water	Score (5 = most important; 1 = least important; n/a = not applicable)			Total score (A + B + C)
	Person A	Person B	Person C	
Taste				
Convenience				
Health benefits				
Cost				
Advertising				

What question(s) will Marcus ask the people he interviews using this questionnaire?

....

Use Marcus's questionnaire to interview three people (A, B and C) in your class. Record your results in each of the relevant columns, and then find a total for each reason by adding the scores. Compare your results with others.

Class discussion

1   What have you learned from your questionnaire results?
2   What did you think was good about Marcus's questionnaire?
3   How could it be improved?

Independent reflection activity

Check your learning goals

If you have achieved them and could teach someone else, put a '★'.

If you have achieved them independently, put a '☺'.

If you can achieve them with support, put a '☺'.

Self-assessment Lessons 4–6

How will I know if I have achieved my learning goals?

Use this activity to reflect on how well you have progressed over the last three lessons.

Tick (✓) 'Achieved independently' if you feel confident that you could apply this skill for yourself.

Tick (✓) 'Achieved with support' if you still need some help when you apply this skill.

If you tick 'Achieved independently', then try to deepen your understanding and provide support for others when working on the next issue.

If you tick 'Achieved with support', look out for opportunities to consolidate this skill when working on the next issue.

Continued

Research learning goals To develop my knowledge and understanding about:	Achieved independently	Achieved with support	I think this because
making questions that can help me investigate an issue, including thinking of questions to ask when interviewing someone			
finding information in sources to answer my own questions			
designing my own questionnaire to use in an investigation			
choosing a suitable way of selecting, organising and recording what I find out			

Issue review

Think about the issue you have been focusing on and complete the following statements.

I was surprised to discover/explore that ....

....

I did not know ....

....

I now think ....

....

7

Getting better at research skills: Lesson 7

Lesson learning goals
These are the goals for this lesson. You will return to this table at the end of the lesson for the independent reflection activity.

My learning goals To get better at:	I think	My teacher/ partner thinks
asking good questions about my issue		
finding good facts to answer my question		

What can I already do?

In Lesson 4, Marcus was developing questions about bottled water:

1 Do you prefer drinking bottled water or tap water?
2 What are the main reasons you prefer bottled water?
3 How much bottled water do you drink every day?
4 What is your favourite drink?

Write down the question number that matches the description.

a An open question that leads to a longer answer. Question ....

b A closed question that has only two possible answers. Question ....

c A question that could lead to a range of possible answers – but these would be one or two words. Question ....

d A question that could lead to a range of possible answers – but these would be numbers/quantities. Question ....

Starter activity

The issue I am focusing on today is:

....

Can you develop a series of questions for the issue you are finding out about and taking action on?

Try to include a range of question types.
Write them in the download that your teacher will give you.

Main activity

Marcus and his group wanted to find out about bottled water in different countries. They wrote to their international school partners. You can read their questions and the answers they received in the download that your teacher will give you.

Use your note-taking skills to summarise their answers in the table. Then answer the questions below:

1   What is similar in all of the children's answers?

....

2   What **significant** differences do you notice?

....

Class discussion

If you wanted to find out more information about the issue and find out ideas that could work where you are, what could you ask?

Think about:

a   An open question that could lead to a longer answer.

....

b   A closed question that would have only two possible answers.

....

c   A question that could lead to a range of possible answers – but these would be one or two words.

....

d   A question that could lead to a range of possible answers – but these should be numbers/quantities.

....

Share your ideas with others in the class.

Independent reflection activity

Check your learning goals
If you have achieved them and could teach someone else, put a '★'.
If you have achieved them independently, put a '☺'.
If you can achieve them with support, put a '☺'.

Getting better at research skills: Lesson 8

Lesson learning goals		
These are the goals for this lesson. You will return to this table at the end of the lesson for the independent reflection activity.		
My learning goals To get better at:	I think	My teacher/ partner thinks
asking questions and writing down answers about them		
picking the most important facts that I have found out about my issue and presenting them clearly		

What can I already do?

Re-read your notes from the Main activity in Lesson 7.

Put a tick (✓) in each row where the statement at the top of the column is correct. Put an ✗ if the statement is incorrect for that person – the first one has been done for you.

	Has a bell in school for drinking water time	Is able to get money back for plastic bottles	Says there is a problem with plastic pollution	Writes about ways plastic is recycled	Writes about ways plastic bottles are reused
Raoul	✗				
Priti	✓				
Hong-Kai	✗				
Afia	✗				
Karin	✗				

Starter activity

The issue I am focusing on today is:

....

Step 1: Read through your notes from Lesson 7 from the five different international partners.

Step 2: Write five questions that can be answered from their responses. Write the questions in the spaces provided in the left-hand column of the table.

Step 3: Choose two respondents and write their names in the top row of the table.

Step 4: Answer the questions for each respondent in note form.

	Respondent 1 Name:	Respondent 2 Name:
Q1		
Q2		
Q3		
Q4		
Q5		

Peer feedback

Show your table to a partner, and ask them to tell you:

Two things that they like about your questions (write what they tell you here):

⭐ ....
....
⭐ ....
....

One thing that you could do better (write what they tell you here):

 ....

Main activity

Now present your **findings**. Use the table you completed in the Starter activity as a plan. Use the sentence starters below to help you.

The issue we have been focusing on is ....

I have been studying the responses of two respondents who live in different parts of the

world, ... and ....

There are some similarities in their responses, firstly ....

In addition, their responses both show that ....

Furthermore, ...

However, there are also differences because ....

For example, ..., whereas ....

Also ....

So, in conclusion, we can see that ....

An idea we could try is ....

Class discussion

Share your ideas with others in the class.

Independent reflection activity

Check your learning goals

If you have achieved them and could teach someone else, put a '★'.

If you have achieved them independently, put a '☺'.

If you can achieve them with support, put a '☺'.

9

Getting better at research skills: Lesson 9

Lesson learning goals
These are the goals for this lesson. You will return to this table at the end of the lesson for the independent reflection activity.

My learning goals To get better at:	I think	My teacher/ partner thinks
giving reasons for choosing a source to help me find out about an issue		
carrying out an investigation and deciding whether a prediction is correct		
choosing a way of clearly showing what I have learned from my research		

What can I already do?

In Lesson 2, you made a prediction about what you would find out from an investigation. Look back and note down your prediction here.

....

In Lesson 3, you carried out that investigation. How would you assess the extent to which your prediction turned out to be accurate? Tick (✓) one box.

Completely accurate	Mostly accurate	Partly accurate	Mostly inaccurate	Completely inaccurate

What reason(s) would you give for your decision?

....

Be ready to share your ideas with the class.

Starter activity

The issue I am focusing on today is:

....

Zara and Arun are doing research into different perspectives on water ownership. A perspective is a viewpoint on an issue based on evidence and reasoning. They'd like to know what different groups of people feel about this issue.

a   Is it better for the water supply to be run by a company that makes a profit?

b   Is it better for the water supply to be run by local government, which gives a subsidy?

Which of the following possible sources of information do you think would be useful for them to use? Tick (✓) the column that you think best describes each source.

	Not useful	Possibly useful	Certainly useful
Carry out a survey to find out how many children have hosepipes at home			
Find out what children in international partner schools think about who runs the water supply where they live and what they think about it			
Look at a local map to see where water is			
Observe children using water			
Talk to children about what they think is the best way to supply water			
Talk to parents to find out how much they pay for water			

Look at the sources you have chosen as 'certainly useful' and tell a partner why you think this.

Main activity

In the download that your teacher will give you, there are eight different ways of clearly showing what has been learned from research.

Each of them has a different use. Can you match the method to its potential use? Write your answers in the download.

Choose three methods that you will use to clearly show what you have learned from your research. Explain why you have chosen each method.

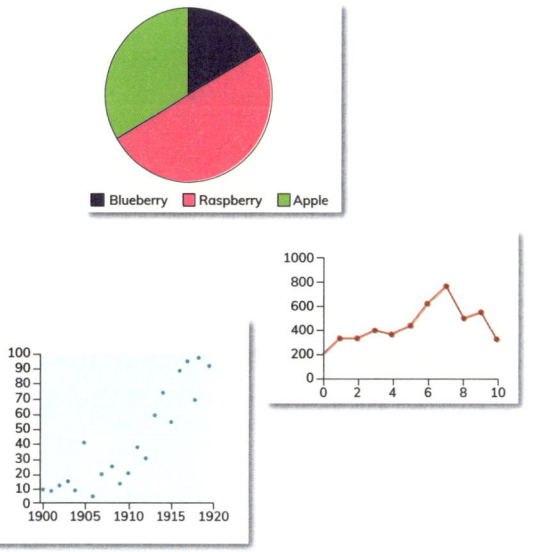

■ Blueberry ■ Raspberry ■ Apple

Method (e.g. pie chart, bar graph)	I have chosen this method because it will help us to...
1	
2	
3	

Class discussion

What methods have you chosen and why?

Share your ideas with others in the class.

Independent reflection activity

Check your learning goals

If you have achieved them and could teach someone else, put a '★'.

If you have achieved them independently, put a '☺'.

If you can achieve them with support, put a '☺'.

Lessons 7–9

How will I know if I have achieved my learning goals?

Use this activity to reflect on how well you have progressed over the last three lessons.

Tick (✓) 'Achieved independently' if you feel confident that you could apply this skill for yourself.

Tick (✓) 'Achieved with support' if you still need some help when you apply this skill.

If you tick 'Achieved independently', then try to deepen your understanding and provide support for others when working on the next issue.

If you tick 'Achieved with support', look out for opportunities to consolidate this skill when working on the next issue.

Continued

Research learning goals To get better at:	Achieved independently	Achieved with support	I think this because
asking good questions about my issue and writing down my answers about them			
finding useful facts from good sources to help me find out about an issue			
carrying out an investigation and deciding whether a prediction is correct			
clearly showing what I have learned from my research			

Reflect on your responses in your self-assessment and identify one area for improvement.

One skill I want to get even better at is:

....

How I will improve:

....

Issue review

Think about the issue you have been focusing on and complete the following statements.

I was surprised to discover/explore that ....

....

I did not know ....

....

I now think ....

....

> Section 2
Analysis

In this section of your Learner's Skills Book you'll be developing your analysis skills while thinking about interesting issues.

But what does analysis involve?

What is your perspective on an issue? Do other people think the same, or do they have a different perspective? Why is the issue happening and how does it affect different people?

Why are other people's perspectives on an issue different from yours and how do they differ?

Can you see any patterns in the information in graphs, charts and tables? How can we improve a local issue?

What causes an issue? How can we improve the issue, based on what we now know from graphs, charts and tables?

Let's start thinking about analysis!

In Section 2: Analysis, you might choose to focus on the Challenge 'How can we stay healthy' and the topic 'Health and wellbeing'.

If you take on this Challenge, you will look at a local health issue. Here are some of the questions you could ask as you carry out your analysis:

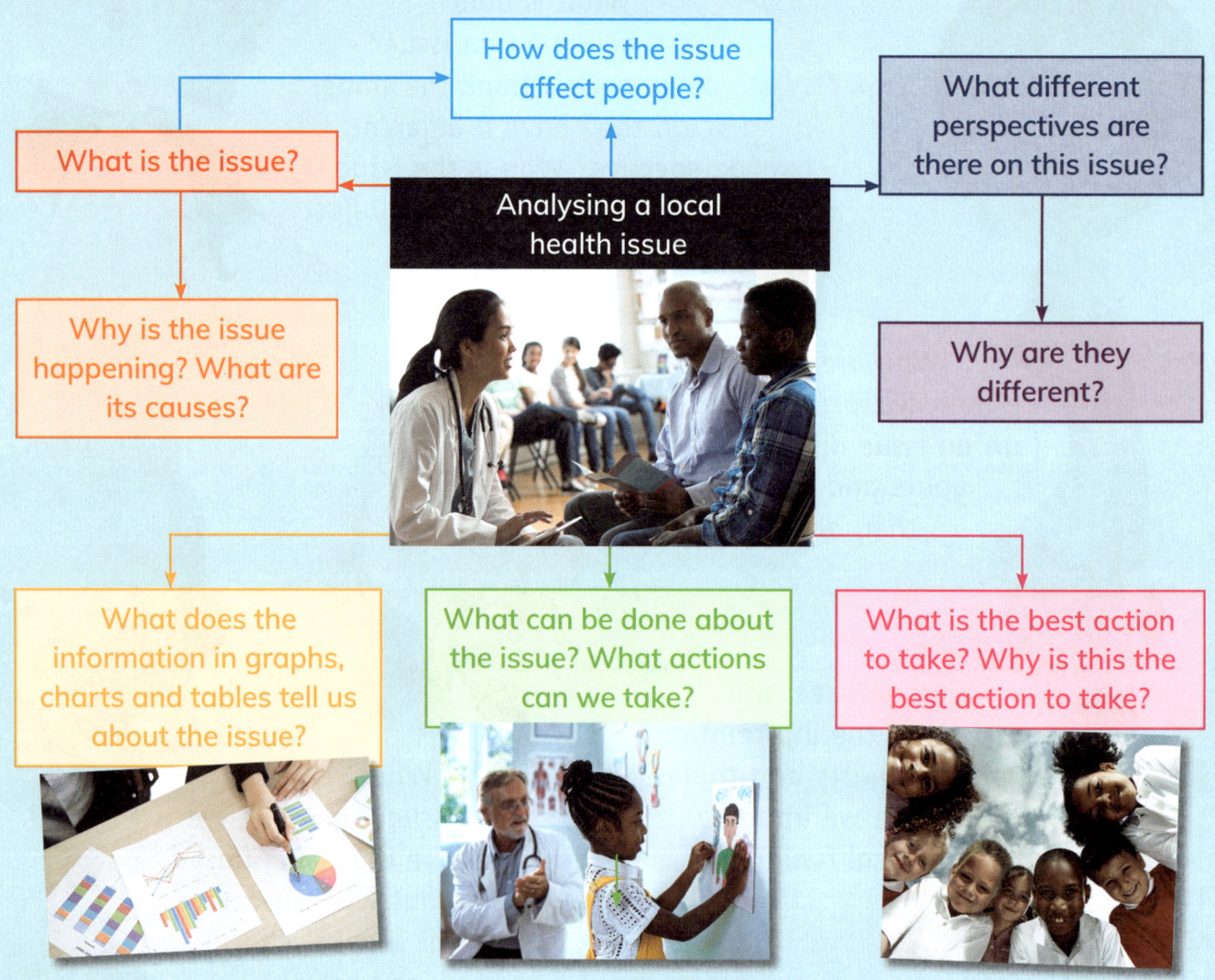

How does the issue affect people?

What different perspectives are there on this issue?

What is the issue?

Analysing a local health issue

Why is the issue happening? What are its causes?

Why are they different?

What does the information in graphs, charts and tables tell us about the issue?

What can be done about the issue? What actions can we take?

What is the best action to take? Why is this the best action to take?

Or you might choose to focus on the topics 'Sport and recreation', 'Water, food and farming' and 'Working with other countries', which you will look at in this section of your Learner's Skills Book.

Think about your answers to these questions:

- What do different people think about an issue?

- Why is the issue happening?
  How does it affect people?

- What can the information in graphs, charts and tables tell us about the issue?

- What can we do about the issue to make it better?

Analysis words

argument	data	infer	perspectives	resolution
causes	disagreement	information	possible	responsible
chart	evidence	limitations	potential	solution
compromise	facts	negotiations	reasons	source
consequences	graph	persuasive	research	table

What is analysis?

Analysis: understanding different perspectives on an issue, its causes and its effects on people

Analysis also includes:

- using information in graphs, charts and tables
- deciding on an action to take
- giving reasons for taking an action

Remember!

You can use any of the Challenges or topics as the starting point to develop your analysis skills. Your teacher may direct you to focus on a specific Challenge or topic, or you may be able to choose for yourself.

1

Starting with analysis skills: Lesson 1

In this chapter you will develop skills in analysis. In general, analysis means looking at something in more detail, for example, in order to understand the different parts that it consists of. In Cambridge Primary Global Perspectives, analysis may involve understanding different perspectives on a topic or issue, or how different causes and consequences are related to one another. Analysis may also involve understanding data presented as numbers or in the form of graphs, charts or tables.

<table>
<tr><td colspan="3">**Lesson learning goals**</td></tr>
<tr><td colspan="3">These are the goals for this lesson.
You will return to this table at the end of the lesson for the independent reflection activity.</td></tr>
<tr><td>**My learning goals**
To start to:</td><td>I think</td><td>My teacher/ partner thinks</td></tr>
<tr><td>recognise that there are differences in the ways different people think about an issue</td><td></td><td></td></tr>
<tr><td>talk about issues that affect people where I live and what causes them</td><td></td><td></td></tr>
</table>

What can I already do?

Public places such as parks are spaces that we share with other people. To try to make sure that everyone can feel safe and enjoy themselves while they are in public places, there are usually rules about how to behave.

In your opinion, what are the three most important rules for people to follow when they are in public places? Write them here:

1 ....

2 ....

3 ....

Talk with a partner. What differences are there between your rules and your partner's? What changes would you like to make now you have compared your rules?

Starter activity

Park Closed

Arun and his friends want to visit their local park, but when they arrive at the entrance, they find that the park is closed to the public because of overcrowding. They talk to some other people who want to use the park. Match the different opinions to the people they speak to (one example has been done for you):

Person	Letter	Opinion
1 Someone who goes to the park to relax	c	a 'Because there are so many people in the park, it's hard to find space to run, but it's still a lot safer than running on the street.'
2 Someone who enjoys looking at nature in the park		b 'The park's the only place where we can all get together and listen to our favourite music as loud as we like!'
3 Someone who takes their daily exercise in the park		c 'These days, you can never find a space where you can sit down that isn't already taken by other people, or covered in litter.'
4 Someone who likes to meet their friends in the park		d 'We love taking our own food and drink to the park, sitting on the grass and having a good chat with all our friends.'
5 Someone who likes to have picnics in the park		e 'With so many visitors every day, the grass, the flowers and the trees in the park are suffering a lot of damage.'

Class discussion

1   Which of the people Arun spoke to would be most in favour of reducing the number of visitors to the park? Why?

2   Different people want to visit the park for different purposes. What **disagreements** between them might there be because of this?

3   What other **reasons** might people have for visiting the park? What would their perspectives be? Remember, a perspective is a viewpoint on an issue based on **evidence** and reasoning.

Main activity

The issue I am focusing on today is:

....

Arun and his friends are talking about the issue at their local park and what they think causes it:

It's a shame the park is closed because of overcrowding, but clearly it is a real issue.

I agree. But why do so many people keep coming to the park? It just makes things worse!

I guess it's because there's nowhere else for people to go where they can get some fresh air.

That's right, we need to open up more public spaces like this so that people can breathe.

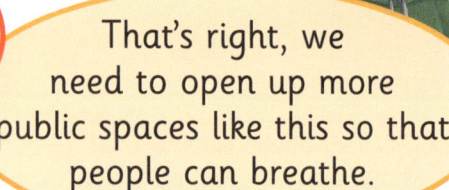

Work in a group. Think of a public place in your local area. What issues are there that affect the people who use this place? Remember, an issue is an important subject or problem for discussion. What causes those issues? Add your ideas to the mind map in the download that your teacher will give you. Then report back to the class.

Class discussion

1   For your chosen public place, what issues are there?
2   What causes these issues?
3   Who are the people who are affected by these issues?
4   What solutions do you think there might be?

Independent reflection activity

Check your learning goals

If you have achieved them and could teach someone else, put a '★'.

If you have achieved them independently, put a '☺'.

If you can achieve them with support, put a '☺'.

2

Starting with analysis skills: Lesson 2

Lesson learning goals		
These are the goals for this lesson. You will return to this table at the end of the lesson for the independent reflection activity.		
My learning goals **To start to:**	I think	My teacher/ partner thinks
find and describe patterns in data and say what they mean		
talk about how a local issue affects me and other people, and what can be done about it		

What can I already do?

Marcus has been thinking about what different park users need in order to enjoy their visit. He uses a Venn diagram to show what each group needs. Complete the diagram. One example has been done for you.

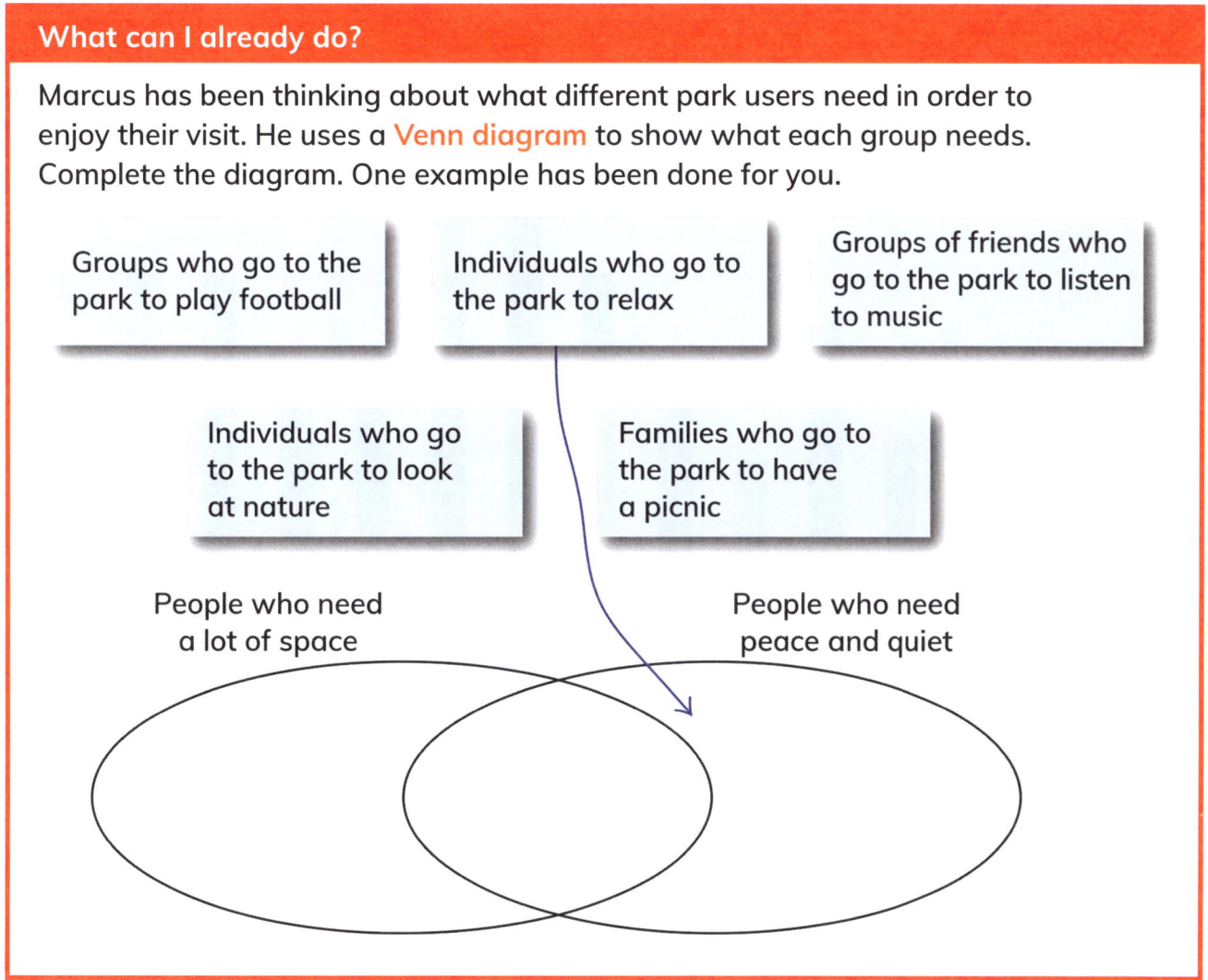

Starter activity

The issue I am focusing on today is:

....

Arun asked the Parks Department (the people in charge of his local park) to share their data about the number of visitors to the park. The Parks Department sent Arun the chart on the next page, showing the number of visitors at different times of the day. The department also told Arun that the maximum number of people visiting the park at any time should not be more than 500 for safety reasons.

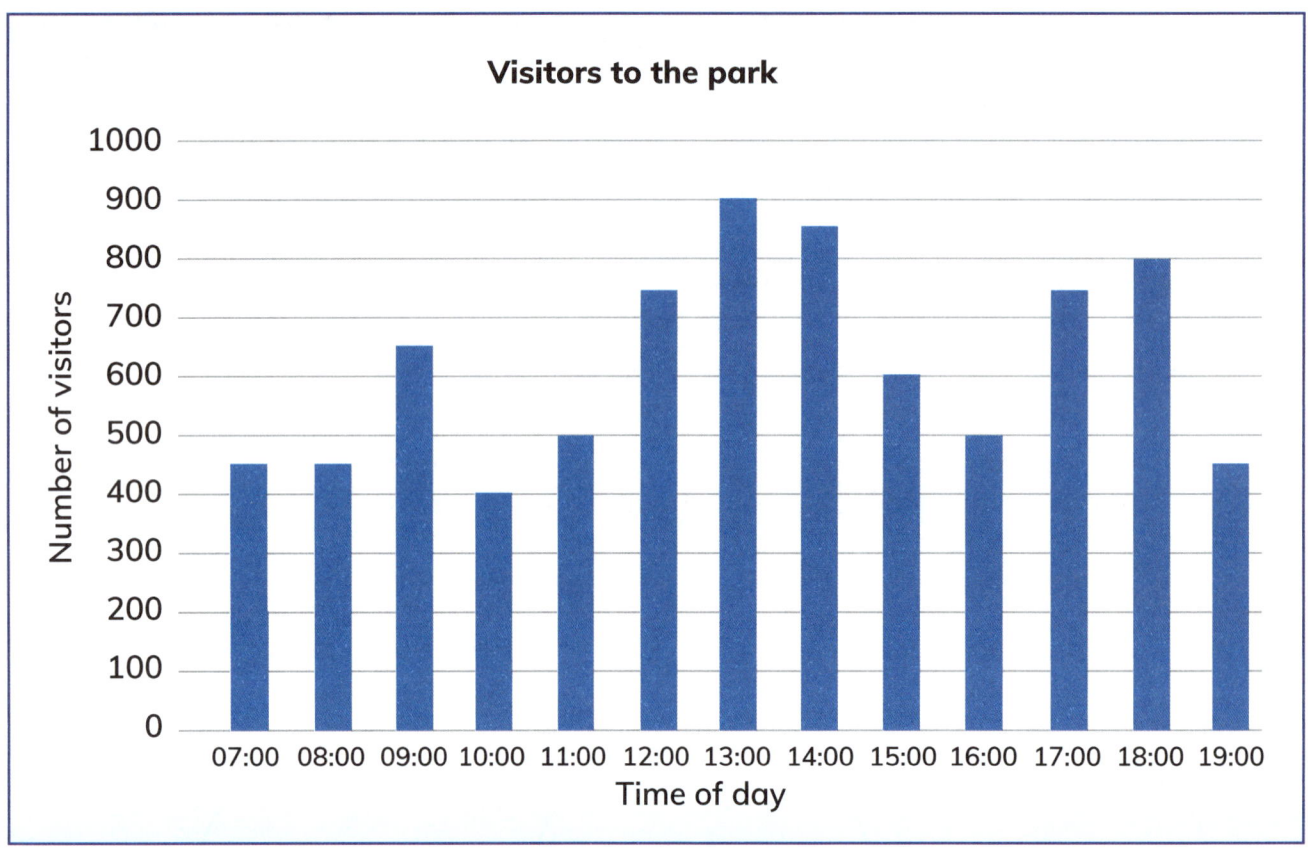

Look at the chart and discuss and answer these questions with a partner:

1 What is the busiest time of day in the park?

   Busiest time: ....

2 What is the least busy time of day?

   Least busy time: ....

3 At what times of day is the number of visitors to the park at or below the maximum safety limit?

   ....

Class discussion

1 Look at the times when the park is most busy.
   Why do you think it is busy at these times?

2 Why is it less busy at other times?

Main activity

The Parks Department also obtained data about two groups of park users: people who picnic in the park and people who exercise in the park. They shared their data with Arun. Your teacher will give you a download containing this information.

Arun and his friends discuss this data.

From 12 o'clock to 2 o'clock, most people in the park are either having a picnic or exercising.

Picnickers always complain that other people disturb them by kicking footballs or because they're running too close to them.

And people who exercise say that picnickers take up too much space and leave their litter behind.

So to reduce overcrowding at the busiest times, perhaps there need to be new rules about exercising and having picnics?

Work in a group. Work out some new rules about picnicking and exercising in the park that would help to solve the issue of overcrowding in the park between 12:00 and 14:00.

Write your solution here.

....

....

....

Peer feedback

Show your solution to someone from another group and ask them to tell you the answers to these questions.

Is the solution likely to solve the issue of overcrowding from 12:00 to 14:00?   Yes/No

Is the solution fair to both the picnickers and the people who want to exercise?   Yes/No

If the answer to either question is 'NO', what changes could you make?

Class discussion

Report your group's solution to the class, explaining how it helps to solve the issue of overcrowding, and how it affects the picnickers and the people doing exercise. Respond to questions from others. Listen to what others tell you about their solutions. Ask questions to find out more.

Independent reflection activity

Check your learning goals
If you have achieved them and could teach someone else, put a '★'.
If you have achieved them independently, put a '☺'.
If you can achieve them with support, put a '☺'.

3

Starting with analysis skills: Lesson 3

<table>
<tr><td colspan="3">Lesson learning goals</td></tr>
<tr><td colspan="3">These are the goals for this lesson.
You will return to this table at the end of the lesson for the independent reflection activity.</td></tr>
<tr><td>My learning goals
To start to:</td><td>I think</td><td>My teacher/
partner thinks</td></tr>
<tr><td>talk about issues that affect people where I live and what causes them</td><td></td><td></td></tr>
<tr><td>talk about how a local issue affects me and other people, and what can be done about it</td><td></td><td></td></tr>
</table>

What can I already do?

Zara has been listening to what two groups of park users are saying about a disagreement between them. The disagreement is between people who go to the park to play football and people who go to the park to look at nature. Match the statements to each group. One example has been done for you.

What they said:

1 'They play their games too near the flower beds and run everywhere.'

2 'We can't enjoy our games because people are always complaining.'

3 'We're upset because plants and trees are being damaged.'

4 'Games of football should be completely banned.'

5 'There should be a separate area in the park just for exercise.'

6 'It's the only green space for nature in the middle of our city.'

7 'The park is the only space where we can get some exercise.'

8 'They want too much space just for plants and trees.'

	Who said it?	
	Football players	Nature lovers
Reason for visiting the park	7	
Cause of the disagreement		
Consequence of the disagreement		
Solution to the disagreement		

Talk with a partner. Which solution do you think would be the fairest?

Starter activity

The issue I am focusing on today is:

....

In the Main activity in Lesson 2, Arun and his friends looked for a solution to the issue of overcrowding in their local park. They discovered a disagreement between two groups of park users: people who want to exercise in the park and people who go to the park to have picnics.

Work in a group. Think of a public place in your local area, and of two different groups of people (Group 1 and Group 2) who want to use that place. What disagreements might there be between the different groups? Choose one disagreement to focus on, and complete the table below:

Where?	Public place:	
Who?	Group 1	Group 2
What is each group's opinion on how to use the public place?		
What are the causes of the disagreement between the two groups?		
What are the consequences of the disagreement?		
What is each group's preferred way of resolving the disagreement?		

Class discussion

Report to the class about the disagreement you have chosen to focus on. Respond to questions from others about the disagreement. Listen to what others tell you about their chosen disagreement. Ask questions to find out more.

Main activity

Work in a group. Decide on the best **resolution** to the disagreement that you have chosen to focus on.

Complete the table below.

Our proposed solution:		
	Group 1	**Group 2**
What does each group gain from our proposal?		
How likely is it that each group would accept our proposal?		
What other groups might be affected by our proposal and how?		

Class discussion

Report to the class about your group's solution. Respond to questions from others. Listen to what others tell you about their solutions. Ask questions to find out more.

Independent reflection activity

Check your learning goals

If you have achieved them and could teach someone else, put a '★'.

If you have achieved them independently, put a '☺'.

If you can achieve them with support, put a '☺'.

Self-assessment Lessons 1–3

How will I know if I have achieved my learning goals?

Use this activity to reflect on how well you have progressed over the last three lessons.

Tick (✓) 'Achieved independently' if you feel confident that you could apply this skill for yourself.

Tick (✓) 'Achieved with support' if you still need some help when you apply this skill.

If you tick 'Achieved independently', then try to deepen your understanding and provide support for others when working on the next issue.

If you tick 'Achieved with support', look out for opportunities to consolidate this skill when working on the next issue.

Analysis learning goals To start to:	Achieved independently	Achieved with support	I think this because
recognise that there are differences in the ways different people think about an issue			
find and describe patterns in data and say what they mean			
talk about issues that affect people where I live and what causes them			
talk about how a local issue affects me and other people, and what can be done about it			

Issue review

Think about the issue you have been focusing on and complete the following statements.

I was surprised to discover/explore that ....

....

I did not know ....

....

I now think ....

....

4

Developing analysis skills: Lesson 4

My learning goals To develop my knowledge and understanding about:	I think	My teacher/ partner thinks
finding and describing patterns in data and saying what they mean		

What can I already do?

Sofia has been making a fact-file about a country she has been researching for a class project. Add the appropriate heading to each piece of information that Sofia has collected. One example has been done for you.

Headings:
Area
Capital ✓
Main crops
Main industries
Maximum/minimum temperatures
Climate
Population

Fact File about East Amberia	
Heading	Fact
1 Capital	Amber City
2	10 025 500
3	1.8 million km²
4	Warm and dry
5	Oil, textiles
6	Cotton, beans, rice
7	32° C (January), 15° C (July)

Talk with a partner. How many of these facts do you know about your country? How is your country different from East Amberia?

Starter activity

The issue I am focusing on today is:

....

Sofia continues her project by reading about two more countries that are neighbours. Read the text below.

'Although Erlandia is larger than Lalandia, it has a smaller population. Most of its 8 million people live in the capital city, which is called Oriel. Much of the country is desert, surrounded by mountains, which makes it unsuitable for farming. This means that Erlandia sometimes experiences food shortages.

Whereas Erlandia covers over 300,000 km², Lalandia has an area of less than 200,000 km². However, it enjoys a better climate, and most of the land is suitable for growing crops. As a result, food products are one of the country's main exports. At just over 20 million, the population of Lalandia is more than double that of Erlandia, and the capital city, Occine, is home to more than 9 million people.

The River Oroc is important to these two nations. It starts in the mountains of Erlandia, flows west through both countries, and is a vital transport link between them.'

Use the information in the text to complete the table below.

	Erlandia	Lalandia
Capital city		
Population		
Area		
Natural features		

Class discussion

1 Which of these two countries would you prefer to live in? Why?

2 What else would you like to find out about the two countries?

Main activity

Work in a group. Your teacher will give you a download containing a source. Share the information in the source with the rest of your group in order to complete the table.

	Erlandia	Lalandia
Climate		
Maximum/minimum temperatures	Maximum Minimum	Maximum Minimum
Top 2 crops	• •	• •
Top 3 industries	• • •	• • •

Class discussion

Erlandia and Lalandia are neighbours.

1   How could the two countries help and support each other?
2   How could each country attract more foreign tourists?

Independent reflection activity

Check your learning goals

If you have achieved them and could teach someone else, put a '★'.

If you have achieved them independently, put a '☺'.

If you can achieve them with support, put a '☺'.

5

Developing analysis skills: Lesson 5

Lesson learning goals		
These are the goals for this lesson. You will return to this table at the end of the lesson for the independent reflection activity.		
My learning goals To develop my knowledge and understanding about:	I think	My teacher/ partner thinks
recognising that there are differences in the ways that different people think about an issue		
talking about issues that affect people where I live and what causes them		

What can I already do?

Marcus is listening to different people giving their opinions on a change that is happening in his local area.

Person A: A lot more traffic will use it, which means there will be more air pollution and noise.

Person B: It will reduce the time it takes to drive from one side of the city to the other.

Person C: There will be lots of jobs for local people while they are constructing it.

Person D: It will encourage more people to use their cars in the city, instead of taking public transport.

Talk with a partner. What is the change that these people are discussing?

Which people have a positive view of the change, and which people have a negative view? What other opinions might there be?

Starter activity

Sofia is investigating how countries can work together to promote sustainability. She sees this headline in a newspaper:

Erlandia to build new dam on River Oroc

Alarm and anger in Lalandia as plans are announced

Sofia reads the report in the newspaper. In the report, different people give their perspectives on the plan to build a new dam. Match the perspectives to the people quoted in the article. One example has been done for you.

1 'The dam can be used to create cheap electricity without burning more fossil fuels. It will mean we can reduce air pollution and help to prevent climate change.'

2 'If water levels in the River Oroc fall as a result of the dam, this will make it harder for ships to use the river. Trade between our two countries will be reduced.'

3 'The dam will have a negative impact on the river's wildlife. For example, fish can no longer migrate to their breeding grounds, and this will affect the local fishing industry.'

4 'If the dam is built, my land will be flooded and my family will have to leave the village where we have lived for generations. I'll have to move to the city and find a new job.'

5 'The dam will mean more water is available for us to grow crops in the desert, using modern irrigation systems. There will be no more food shortages!'

6 'The water level in our part of the river will fall because of the dam, and this will mean a much smaller harvest. Cotton and rice need a lot of water!'

a Environmental campaigner, Lalandia   3   d Minister of Transport, Lalandia   ☐

b Farmer, Erlandia   ☐   e Farmer, Lalandia   ☐

c Minister of Agriculture, Erlandia   ☐   f Environmental campaigner, Erlandia   ☐

Class discussion

1 Which of the people are for the dam, and which are against?

2 What other people might have a perspective on the new dam?

3 What do you think their perspective would be? Try to think of some perspectives that are for the dam and some that are against.

Main activity

The issue I am focusing on today is:

....

Sofia and her friends are discussing a change that is taking place in their local area.

The plan to build a new supermarket has upset some of the local shopkeepers, who might go out of business.

That's not all. People who live nearby are worried about the increased traffic it will bring to the area.

Some people say that the supermarket will bring more jobs to the area, so it's a good thing.

And it will sell things more cheaply than the local shops, and offer a wider variety of goods.

Work in a group. Think of something that has changed (or a change that is being planned) in your local area.

Who is affected by this change? Are they affected in a negative or a positive way? What would their perspective on the change be?

Your teacher will give you a download containing four speech bubbles for you to fill in. Use the speech bubbles to show four different perspectives on the change from four different people. Try to include a balance of positive and negative views.

Peer feedback

Show your work to a partner from a different group, and ask them to answer these questions:

Have you shown the perspectives of four different types of people?   Yes/No

Is there a balance of positive and negative views about the change?   Yes/No

If the answer to any of the questions is 'NO', what changes could you make?

Class discussion

Report to the class about the local change you have chosen to focus on, and the different perspectives that people have on it. Respond to questions from others about the change. Listen to what others tell you about the change they have chosen. Ask questions to find out more.

Independent reflection activity

Check your learning goals

If you have achieved them and could teach someone else, put a '★'.

If you have achieved them independently, put a '☺'.

If you can achieve them with support, put a '☺'.

6

Developing analysis skills: Lesson 6

What can I already do?

Two of Zara's neighbours are having a disagreement:

- Neighbour A complains that Neighbour B plays loud music late at night.
- Neighbour B's window has been broken, and Neighbour B believes that Neighbour A's children are responsible because they like playing football outside.

Talk with a partner. What do you think the two neighbours should do in order to resolve their disagreement? What changes could each neighbour make?

Starter activity

The issue I am focusing on today is:

....

Sofia looks at a map to try to understand the impact that the new dam in Erlandia will have.

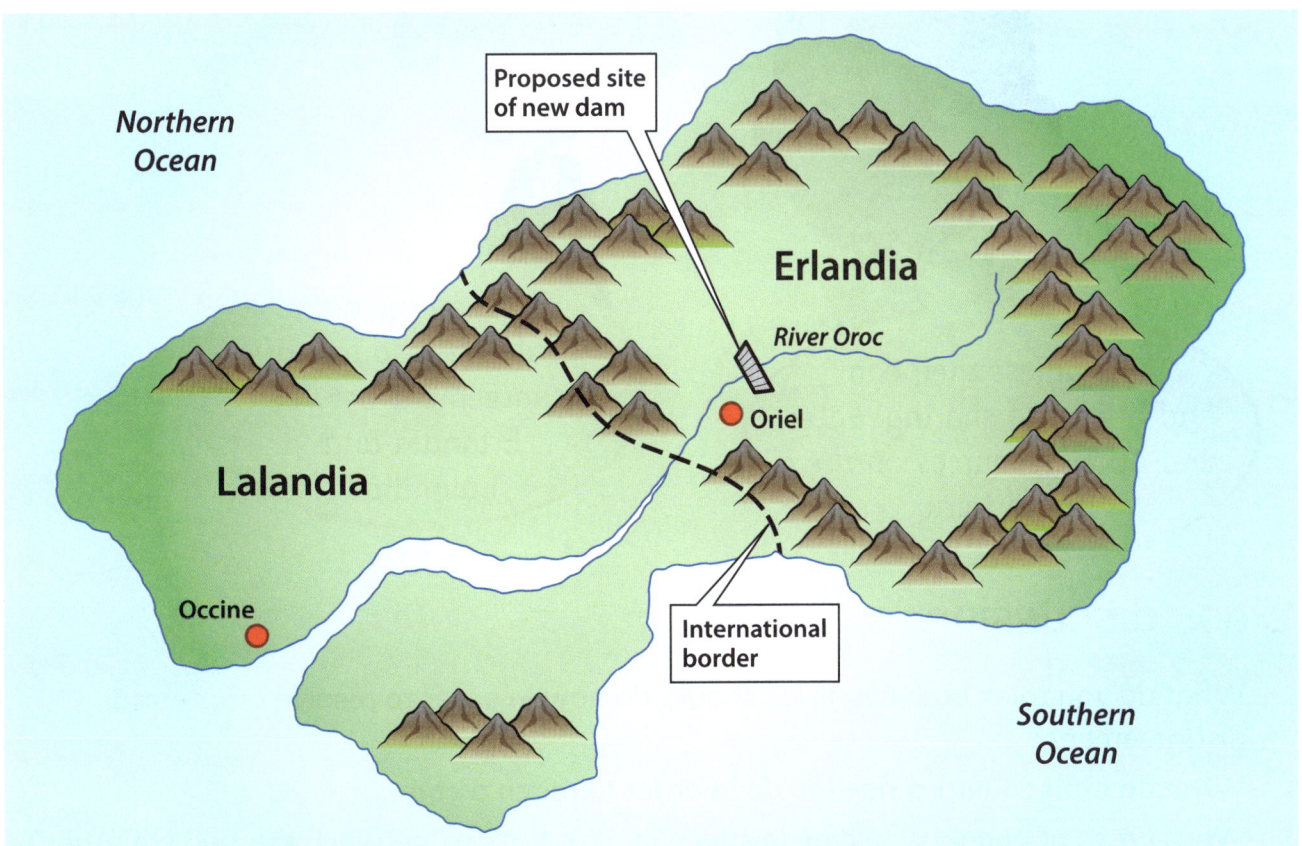

Sofia talks with her friends about the situation. Read what they say, and think about your answers to the questions that follow:

As I see it, Erlandia has much to gain from building the dam, but Lalandia has a lot to lose.

Erlandia needs more water, but the dam will restrict the amount of water that Lalandia gets from the river.

Yes, unless they can find a way of sharing water and other resources on their island fairly.

So the new dam could be a source of disagreement between Erlandia and Lalandia?

Class discussion

1 What do you think both countries should do now in order to resolve a potential disagreement?

2 What do both countries need to do in order to reach a compromise?

3 What types of people would be involved in negotiations between the two countries?

Main activity

Work in a group. You are going to hold a conference with the others in your group in order to try to resolve the potential disagreement between Erlandia and Lalandia over the building of the dam. Your teacher will give you a role-card. Read your card and think about what you will say at the conference in order to help reach an agreement between the two sides.

Now hold your conference with the other members of your group, taking it in turns to speak.

Class discussion

Report to the class about the results of your conference. Respond to questions from others. Listen to what others tell you about the results of their conference. Ask questions to find out more.

Independent reflection activity

Check your learning goals

If you have achieved them and could teach someone else, put a '★'.

If you have achieved them independently, put a '☺'.

If you can achieve them with support, put a '☺'.

Self-assessment Lessons 4–6

How will I know if I have achieved my learning goals?

Use this activity to reflect on how well you have progressed over the last three lessons.

Tick (✓) 'Achieved independently' if you feel confident that you could apply this skill for yourself.

Tick (✓) 'Achieved with support' if you still need some help when you apply this skill.

If you tick 'Achieved independently', then try to deepen your understanding and provide support for others when working on the next issue.

Continued

If you tick 'Achieved with support', look out for opportunities to consolidate this skill when working on the next issue.

Analysis learning goals To develop my knowledge and understanding about:	Achieved independently	Achieved with support	I think this because
finding and describing patterns in data and saying what they mean			
recognising that there are differences in the ways that different people think about an issue			
talking about issues that affect people where I live and what causes them			
talking about how a local issue affects me and other people, and what can be done about it			

Issue review

Think about the issue you have been focusing on and complete the following statements.

I was surprised to discover/explore that ....

....

I did not know ....

....

I now think ....

....

7

Getting better at analysis skills: Lesson 7

Lesson learning goals		
These are the goals for this lesson. You will return to this table at the end of the lesson for the independent reflection activity.		
My learning goals To get better at:	I think	My teacher/ partner thinks
identifying some different ways that people can think about an issue		
recognising words that show the strength of feeling about an issue		

What can I already do?

Arun and the group have been discussing an issue in their local area. They want to know if the group is clear on what the issue is. They want to understand what different people think. They want to make up their own minds on the issue.

Arun: I get what the issue is. The issue is whether or not the new supermarket they want to build will bring more jobs to the area.

Zara: I'm very clear what different people think. People who live near me are really worried about the increased traffic. District 7 people aren't so bothered.

Sofia: I know what I think. Our local shops will go out of business. They use less plastic. I don't want this to go ahead.

Marcus: I'm clear on the issue; not so clear where I stand. My auntie runs a shop. She doesn't think her business will lose customers.

Read the following statements and assess your current level of understanding. Tick (✓) the answer that best applies to you:

1 I know an issue that people disagree about in my local area.

I am very clear	I am quite clear	I have some idea	I am not very clear

2 I know what different people think about the issue.

I am very clear	I am quite clear	I have some idea	I am not very clear

3 I know what I think about the issue.

I am very clear	I am quite clear	I have some idea	I am not very clear

Hold a class discussion: How could we improve our scores?

Starter activity

The issue I am focusing on today is:

....

Your teacher will give you some different perspectives on the dam project. How would you categorise them? The first one has been done for you.

View	Strongly against	Somewhat against	Neutral	Somewhat in favour	Strongly in favour
1	✓				
2					
3					
4					
5					
6					

Class discussion

Look again at your answers in the table and discuss these questions:

1 How did you recognise an argument that was strongly against the dam?

2 What words or phrases did the person making the argument use to emphasise the strength of their feelings?

3 How did you recognise an argument that was strongly in favour of the dam?

4 What words or phrases did the person making the argument use to emphasise the strength of their feelings?

5 What words or phrases could you use to emphasise the strength of your feelings about an issue?

Main activity

Look back and choose two of the people you identified in the Main activity of Lesson 5. Each had a different perspective on an issue.

1 What was the issue?

Mine was whether or not to build a new supermarket – what was yours?

....

....

2 What was the first person's perspective?

....

....

Mine was the perspective of the manager of the development **company**, 'The area has been waiting for years for this!'

3 What facts could the first person use to convince someone to support their perspective?

Mine said 'around 150 new permanent jobs'.

....

....

4 What words or phrases could the first person use to convince someone that they ought to care about the issue?

....

....

I got 'transform a derelict site . . . a modern and high-quality . . . **significant contribution** to the local economy . . . **vibrant** development . . . secure employment.'

5   What was the second person's perspective?

Mine was a community **campaigner**.

....

....

6   What facts could the second person use to convince someone to support their perspective?

....

....

I got 'Money spent in a local shop will stay in the local area; money spent in a supermarket won't.'

7   What words or phrases could the second person use to convince someone that they ought to care about the issue?

I got 'decimated local sports and leisure facilities . . . Negative traffic impact. . . Community voices ignored.'

....

....

Peer feedback

Pretend you are one of the people and try to convince your partner to support your perspective on the issue, and ask them to tell you:

Two things that they like about your **persuasive** powers (write what they tell you here):

★ ....

★ ....

One thing that you could do better (write what they tell you here):

....

Independent reflection activity

Check your learning goals

If you have achieved them and could teach someone else, put a '★'.

If you have achieved them independently, put a '☺'.

If you can achieve them with support, put a '☺'.

8

Getting better at analysis skills: Lesson 8

Lesson learning goals		
These are the goals for this lesson. You will return to this table at the end of the lesson for the independent reflection activity.		
My learning goals **To get better at:**	I think	My teacher/ partner thinks
developing ideas about how I would solve a local issue		
considering pros and cons for different people about ways to solve a local issue		

What can I already do?

Sofia has been making connections between what she has found out and her own perspective on an issue:

> The action I support to resolve this issue is to stop the supermarket development. I want our local shops to stay. I think that people in our area should have more shops where they can buy things grown and made in the community. I feel passionate about this because I love my area, and I really don't enjoy the big companies coming in to take over and making it look just the same as everywhere else. I know that when people shop locally, the money stays locally.

Prepare your ideas for a class discussion.

1   What is Sofia's issue?
2   What is Sofia's perspective about the issue?
3   What does she think should be done?
4   Why does she think or feel this way?
5   What facts have made her think or feel this way?
6   If she wanted to convince someone else to support her perspective, what could she say?
7   If someone wanted to convince someone to support the opposite perspective to Sofia's, what could they say?

Be ready to justify your ideas.

Starter activity

The issue I am focusing on today is:

....

Arun wants to focus on a new supermarket being built. Use Arun's examples
to help you write sentences about a different local issue you want to investigate.

1   What is your issue?

Mine is why the supermarket *should* be built

....

....

2   What is your own personal perspective about the issue?
    How do you feel about it?

....

....

I'm *for* it. I think it would be a positive thing for the area.

3   What do you think should be done?

The council should agree the plans for the supermarket – and the houses they promise to build with it.

....

....

....

4   Why do you think or feel this way?

....

....

Jobs are really important. If someone can't find work it can bring misery to a whole family.

5   What facts have made you think or feel this way?

The site has been **derelict** for years. There will be over 150 full-time secure jobs at the new supermarket.

....

....

....

6   If you wanted to convince someone else to support your perspective, what would your key points be?

- District 5 – been waiting for too long (20+ years) for the site to be developed
- It is a waste ground
- At last there is a clear business plan for our area
- Will bring not only jobs (150 permanent), but also housing (75+)
- Now is the time to bring new life into our community!

....
....
....
....
....
....
....

Main activity

Now it is your turn. Choose an issue with other members of your group. Think of a possible solution. Consider the impacts on different groups of people. Record your own thoughts by answering the following questions.

To help you here are Sofia's answers for her issue.

1   Whose perspectives would probably be favourable to your solution?

Stopping the supermarket
1.   Local community activists. Local shopkeepers. People who don't mind shopping a few times each week.
2.   We need to get better links with local farms – maybe set up a local buying group.
3.   People who are used to driving to a big supermarket once a week will need to change their habits.
4.   Think of the planet! You don't need food grown that far away. Local food is tastier because it is picked fresher.

....
....

2   Would your solution be effective?

....
....

3   How would this solution change the way different groups of people might have
    to behave?

    ....

    ....

    ....

4   How could you justify your solution to people who might not want to change the way
    they behave at first? (Think about different global and local perspectives on the issue.)

    ....

    ....

    ....

Class discussion

Listen to the other groups' issues and their solutions.

1   Do you agree with their solutions?

    ....

2   What are the pros and cons?

    ....

3   What perspectives on the issue can you think of?

    ....

Be ready to report back to the class.

Independent reflection activity

Check your learning goals

If you have achieved them and could teach someone else, put a '★'.

If you have achieved them independently, put a '☺'.

If you can achieve them with support, put a '☺'.

9

Getting better at analysis skills: Lesson 9

These are the goals for this lesson.
You will return to this table at the end of the lesson for the independent reflection activity.

My learning goals To get better at:	I think	My teacher/ partner thinks
describing in some detail the differences in the ways people think about an issue		
finding connections between the causes of an issue and its consequences for different people		
using a pattern found in data to support an argument for a course of action and explaining why		

What can I already do?

Look back to Arun's data from the Parks Department about two groups of park users from people who picnic in the park and people who exercise in the park. It was in the Starter activity in Lesson 2, but your teacher will give it to you again as a download.

Here are some statements about the data. First decide if any are false. Put '✗' against any that you think are *definitely* false. Now look at the other statements. How sure can we be about them? Put 'L' and a tick '✓' against any that you think are *likely* explanations. Put 'P' and a tick '✓' against any that you think are *possible* explanations – but we can't be so sure.

a   People do not have picnics before 10:00.

b   18:00 is a popular time for picnics.

c   07:00–10:00 is a popular time for exercise.

d   The time that the park is at its busiest is 13:00.

e   The reason people visit the park in the middle of the day is because there is nowhere else that is pleasant to be during their lunch break.

Starter activity

Arun's group thought of different solutions to their local issue about park overcrowding.

They decided to conduct a survey. Under supervision, they asked 50 children and 50 adults which proposed solution they favoured most. The results are shown in the following table.

	Solution	Children	Adults	Total in favour
1	Do nothing. Leave it to people's common sense.	12	27	39
2	Ban group exercise in the park (for example, games of football) between 12:00 and 15:00.	3	7	10
3	Allow people to have picnics only in special areas, where there are litter/recycling bins.	11	4	15
4	Ban dog walking in the park between 12:00 and 15:00.	12	0	12
5	Restrict sports events to 50 participants.	1	3	4
6	Make organisers pay for using the park to play sport.	1	0	1
7	Drain the lake to make more space for sport.	0	1	1
8	Remove the playground to make more space for sport.	0	1	1
9	Close the cafe between 12:00 and 15:00.	3	0	3
10	Close the High Street to traffic and build picnic tables there.	7	7	14
	Total surveyed	**50**	**50**	

What do we know **for sure** from the survey results? What can we reasonably infer (work out using the available evidence) about what causes disagreements in the park? What can we reasonably infer about the consequences of overcrowding? Add your ideas to the table that your teacher will give you.

Class discussion

Share your thoughts with the class.

Main activity

Zara, Arun, Sofia and Marcus have been discussing the results of their data and using it to decide what should be done next. You can read their ideas on the download that your teacher will give you.

Use the table below to analyse their suggestions.
The first one has been done for you.

Name	Gave a global reason for their action.	Considered different local perspectives.	Referred to the survey data.	Considered potential strengths of the action.	Considered potential weaknesses of the action.
Zara	✗	✗	✓	✗	✓
Arun					
Marcus					
Sofia					

Now either write a justification for the action you are considering as part of the issue you are focusing on or write a justification for an action you think that the local government in Arun, Zara, Sofia and Marcus's area should take. It does not have to be one that the team have thought of already.

The issue I am focusing on today is:

....

My proposed action is ....

....

This action would be a positive change because ....

....

I know that different people would benefit from this action because ....

....

The benefits of this approach would be, firstly, that ....

....

In addition, ...

....

There are limitations to this approach because ....

....

However, overall, it can be seen that ....

....

Independent reflection activity

Check your learning goals

If you have achieved them and could teach someone else, put a '★'.

If you have achieved them independently, put a '☺'.

If you can achieve them with support, put a '☹'.

Self-assessment Lessons 7–9

How will I know if I have achieved my learning goals?

Use this activity to reflect on how well you have progressed over the last three lessons.

Tick (✓) 'Achieved independently' if you feel confident that you could apply this skill for yourself.

Tick (✓) 'Achieved with support' if you still need some help when you apply this skill.

If you tick 'Achieved independently', then try to deepen your understanding and provide support for others when working on the next issue.

If you tick 'Achieved with support', look out for opportunities to consolidate this skill when working on the next issue.

Continued

Analysis learning goals To get better at:	Achieved independently	Achieved with support	I think this because
describing differences in the ways that people think about an issue			
recognising words that show the strength of feeling about an issue			
finding and interpreting patterns in data			
suggesting a course of action to help solve a local issue and explaining my reasons			
finding connections between the causes of an issue and its consequences for different people			

Reflect on your responses in your self-assessment and identify one area for improvement.

One skill I want to get even better at is:

....

How I will improve:

....

Issue review

Think about the issue you have been focusing on and complete the following statements.

I was surprised to discover/explore that ....

....

I did not know ....

....

I now think ....

....

> Section 3
Evaluation

In this section of your Learner's Skills Book you'll be developing your evaluation skills while thinking about interesting issues.

But what does evaluation involve?

What perspective do sources present? Do you agree or disagree with what your source says?

Who created this source and what is their purpose? Is the source useful in helping you to understand more about an issue?

How useful is a source of information for understanding an issue? What are its strengths and weaknesses? How up-to-date is the information in the source?

Which points do you agree or disagree with in the source?

Let's start thinking about evaluation!

In Section 3: Evaluation, you might choose to focus on the Challenge 'How are countries different?' and the topic 'Working with other countries'.

If you take on this Challenge, you and your group may want to discuss which sources of information are most helpful when comparing two countries, and choose those sources which you think will be most accurate and reliable. Here are some of the sources you could use:

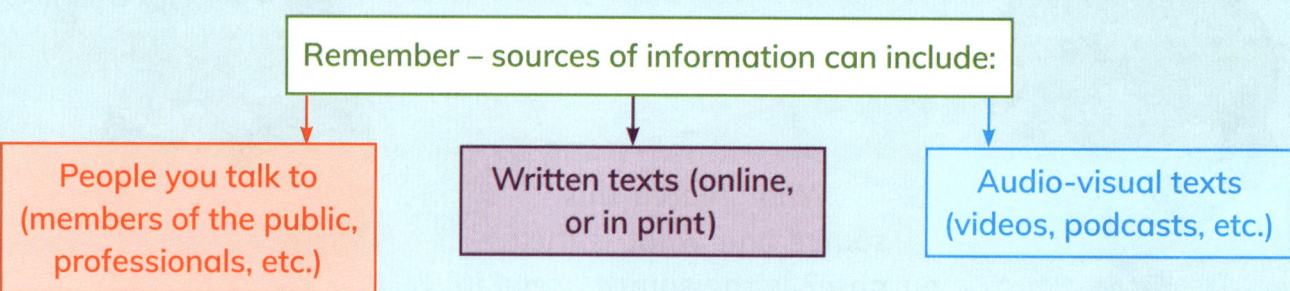

Remember – sources of information can include:

| People you talk to (members of the public, professionals, etc.) | Written texts (online, or in print) | Audio-visual texts (videos, podcasts, etc.) |

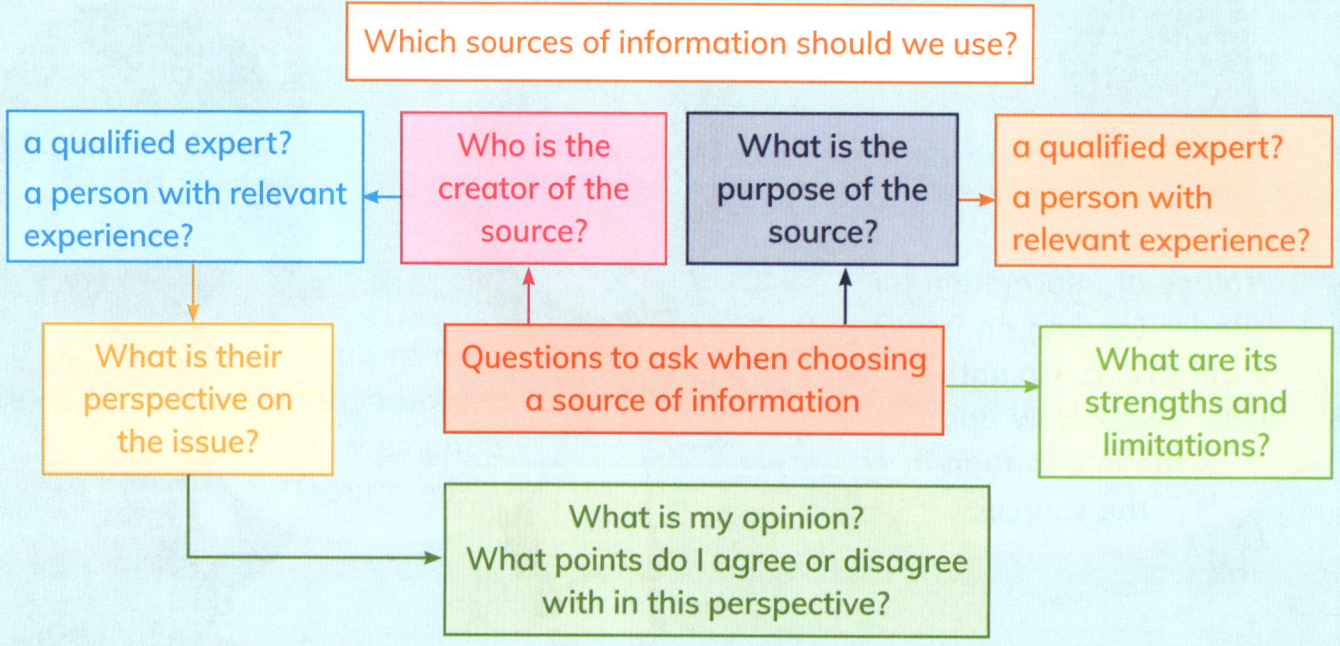

Which sources of information should we use?

a qualified expert?
a person with relevant experience?

Who is the creator of the source?

What is the purpose of the source?

a qualified expert?
a person with relevant experience?

What is their perspective on the issue?

Questions to ask when choosing a source of information

What are its strengths and limitations?

What is my opinion?
What points do I agree or disagree with in this perspective?

Or you might choose to focus on the topics 'Obeying the law', 'Looking after planet Earth', and 'Water, food and farming', which are explored in this section of your Learner's Skills Book.

Think about your answers to these questions:

- Who created the source?

- Why did they create the source?

- What are the strengths and limitations of the source?

- What is my opinion of the perspective presented in the source?

- What points do I agree or disagree with?

Evaluation words

argument	information	perspective	research
author	limitations	persuasive	source
fact	opinions	purpose	strengths

What is evaluation?

Evaluation: choosing sources of information which will be useful when you need to understand more about an issue

Evaluation also includes:

- discussing who created the source of information, and why

- talking about the strengths and limitations of a source

- giving your opinion of the perspective presented in a source, saying what you agree or disagree with

Remember!

You can use any of the Challenges or topics as the starting point to develop your evaluation skills. Your teacher may direct you to focus on a specific Challenge or topic, or you may be able to choose for yourself.

Starting with evaluation skills: Lesson 1

In this chapter you will develop skills in evaluation. To evaluate something means to consider or study something carefully and decide how good or bad it is.

Lesson learning goals

These are the goals for this lesson.
You will return to this table at the end of the lesson for the independent reflection activity.

My learning goals To start to:	I think	My teacher/ partner thinks
discuss the author and purpose of a source		
recognise why a source may be useful		
say what I think about someone else's perspective		

What can I already do?

Sofia and Marcus have been thinking about their Cambridge Primary Global Perspectives topic on 'Obeying the law'. They were talking about sources of information they used.

Sofia: We found out how laws are made. A local politician gave us a talk. We read a history book.

Marcus: The politician told us about new laws she wants. The history book told us about the first police officers.

Talk to a partner about a topic or issue you have studied – remember, an issue is an important subject or problem for discussion – and what sources of information you have used.

Starter activity

Marcus, Sofia, Arun and Zara's class collected sources of information about their topic on 'Obeying the law' and made a list. They thought about who wrote each source and what its purpose was.

Source	Author	Purpose
Talk to our school	A local politician	To tell us information about what she does in her job To give her perspective about new laws
Newspaper report	Court correspondent	To give information about a robbery in our town: what the crime was, what the judge said, the punishment
Our Class Charter	Our class	To make sure we know our rights in our class and to set out our responsibilities
Advert	A local law firm	To tell people about what kind of law work they do and to give contact information
Convention on the rights of the child	The United Nations	To tell us all about our rights To explain what governments have to do
History book	A famous historian	To give information about cruel punishment in the past To tell us how the law changed
Letter to the local newspaper	Mozahar Hossain	To give us the author's perspective about a change in the law
Letter from our international partner school	Correspondent from our international partner school	To answer our question about their Class Charter To tell us about what their government was doing about the UN Convention on the rights of the child
Newspaper foreign news section	Correspondents in different countries	To give readers information about law enforcement in different countries

The issue I am focusing on today is:

....

Your teacher will give you a similar table as a download. List the sources of information that you have available about your topic or issue. Summarise your understanding of who wrote each source and what each source is for.

Main activity

Sofia, Marcus, Arun and Zara have been evaluating these sources of information for their topic. They were looking for sources with a global perspective. They ranked them in a 'diamond nine'.

Most useful

Source: UN Convention on the rights of the child
Useful points: The UN works all around the world
Limitations: Not clear on how it is working here

Source: Letter from our international partner school
Useful points: We can compare our class to theirs
Limitations: Only their perspective

Source: Newspaper foreign news section
Useful points: News from different countries with different laws
Limitations: Only writes about things that are going wrong

Source: Talk from a politician
Useful points: Making laws is her job
Limitations: Didn't really talk about other countries

Source: Our class charter
Useful points: We have a responsibility to the environment
Limitations: It is by and for our class – not a wide perspective

Source: Advert for a law firm
Useful points: They do deal with refugees from different countries
Limitations: No info – only contact details

Source: History book
Useful points: It gives a perspective on law in the past
Limitations: Focuses on our country

Source: Letter to the local newspaper
Useful points: It gives a perspective on how the law should change
Limitations: Focuses on our area

Source: Newspaper report about a robbery in our town
Useful points: It gives a perspective on how the law works in a real case
Limitations: Focus is on our town only

Least useful

The UN convention *has* to go top. It is global and I agree with what it says. These are our rights and *every* child's too!

You're right, Sofia; it is massively important. But we do also need to know how rights are respected here too.

Evaluate the sources of information you have for your topic or issue. Look for sources with a global perspective. Share your thoughts on each source in your group. Rank them in a 'diamond nine' in the template that your teacher will give you.

Now look at the sources that you have ranked in your diamond nine. What points does each one make? Do you agree or disagree with these points? Make two lists.

Class discussion

Your teacher will play a guessing game with you about some familiar texts.

Be ready to ask questions about:

- the author of each text
- the purpose of each text
- the points made in the text.

Independent reflection activity

Check your learning goals

If you have achieved them and could teach someone else, put a '★'.

If you have achieved them independently, put a '☺'.

If you can achieve them with support, put a '☺'.

2

Starting with evaluation skills: Lesson 2

Lesson learning goals		
These are the goals for this lesson. You will return to this table at the end of the lesson for the independent reflection activity.		
My learning goals To start to:	I think	My teacher/ partner thinks
say what I think about someone else's perspective		

What can I already do?

Arun: The opposite is true. Can anyone now seriously dispute the positive benefits?

Zara: These shy mammals are sometimes seen . . .

Sofia: Having understood this, I think it is absolutely imperative for all reasonable people now to . . .

Marcus: His heart was ablaze; ablaze because he knew exactly what was next.

Two of the team are saying what they think about someone else's perspective. The other two are speaking for different purposes. Which two do you think are saying what they think about someone else's perspective? How do you know? Be ready to share your ideas in the class discussion.

Starter activity

The issue I am focusing on today is:

....

An **argument** is a series of statements containing **reasons** and **evidence** which support a claim about an issue. When you are writing an argument, you need to be able to make it clear to your audience or readers whether you are **for** or **against** something. It is often the case that we need to put forward our perspective if something is going to change, and we want things to stay as they are. It is also often true that we need to put forward our perspective because something has remained the way it is for a long time, and we feel that it is time for a change.

Zara has picked out some phrases from people's perspectives. They were discussing the issue of whether or not a law should be changed. Which ones do you think she found in arguments for the change? Which ones do you think she found in *arguments* against the change? Discuss your responses with a partner.

	For (✓) or against (✗)
There is clearly an urgent need for this law.	
It is completely unnecessary to . . .	
There is a growing understanding that the current situation simply cannot be allowed to continue.	
The citizens of this country know how to exercise common sense.	
If we fail to take this step, how will history judge us?	

Main activity

Sofia looked in detail at a text. The issue is a change to international law – your teacher will give you the perspective on the issue that she has been reading. She has been picking out the main ideas, which she has highlighted in yellow. She has also been picking out the phrases that show that the writer's perspective on the issue is for a change, which she has highlighted in green.

Your teacher will give you the work she has done so far – can you finish her summary?

Class discussion

When someone puts forward their perspective, how can you spot weak arguments? What does a strong argument to support a perspective need?

Poor arguments aren't **logical**.

Good arguments usually have clear evidence backing them up.

Good arguments can encourage you to think differently. They help you understand things in a new way.

Weak arguments just state things and expect you to agree.

Peer feedback

Swap books with a partner.

Ask them to look at your work in Lessons 1 and 2 and finish these sentences, then sign their name:

You successfully commented on the author and/or purpose of a source when you

....

You successfully commented on the useful points and/or limitations of a source when you

....

You showed that you understood what the main perspective of a source was when you

....

Signed

....

Independent reflection activity

Check your learning goals

If you have achieved them and could teach someone else, put a '★'.

If you have achieved them independently, put a '☺'.

If you can achieve them with support, put a '☹'.

Self-assessment Lessons 1–2

How will I know if I have achieved my learning goals?

Use this activity to reflect on how well you have progressed over the last two lessons.

Tick (✓) 'Achieved independently' if you feel confident that you could apply this skill for yourself.

Tick (✓) 'Achieved with support' if you still need some help when you apply this skill.

Continued

If you tick 'Achieved independently', then try to deepen your understanding and provide support for others when working on the next issue.

If you tick 'Achieved with support', look out for opportunities to consolidate this skill when working on the next issue.

Evaluation learning goals To start to:	Achieved independently	Achieved with support	I think this because
discuss the author and purpose of a source			
say what I think about someone else's perspective			

Issue review

Think about the issue you have been focusing on and complete the following statements.

I was surprised to discover/explore that ....

....

I did not know ....

....

I now think ....

....

Developing evaluation skills: Lesson 3

These are the goals for this lesson.
You will return to this table at the end of the lesson for the independent reflection activity.

My learning goals To develop my knowledge and understanding about:	I think	My teacher/ partner thinks
considering the author and purpose of a source		
identifying the strengths and limitations of a source		
discussing the perspective of a source		

What can I already do?

Zara and Arun have been thinking about their Cambridge Primary Global Perspectives topic on 'Obeying the law'. They were talking about sources of information they used.

When we found out the date that the police service was set up, that was a **fact**. You can check this.

When the politician told us about the new law that she wants, that was her perspective. You can disagree.

Talk to a partner about a topic or issue you have studied. Try to identify a fact that you found out and a perspective. Remember, a perspective is a viewpoint on an issue based on evidence and reasoning. Be ready to share your ideas in a class discussion.

Starter activity

In Marcus and Zara's class, they have been thinking about ways they can evaluate the **strengths** and limitations of sources and perspectives for their Global Perspectives topic on 'Obeying the law'. They made a list of questions.

Individual sources are not going to give us everything we want on their own!

- Does the author address our issue?
- Is the author in a good position to comment on our issue?
- Is there anything important that the author has left out?
- Are we clear about the author's perspective?
- Are we given clear local perspectives?
- Does it consider a global perspective on the issue?
- Is the source one-sided?
- Does it give us a clear perspective about what action needs to be taken?
- What points do we agree or disagree with?

Arun and Sofia have found a source from the *Westside Observer*, a local newspaper.

The group have been working out what the author's perspective on the issue is.

You can read the source and the group's comments in the download that your teacher will give you.

Now it is over to you. Can you help the team by summarising their discussion? Use the table in the download to do this.

Main activity

The issue I am focusing on today is:

....

Now discuss a source for your issue in your group.

Can you summarise your discussion? Use the table to help you.

Who wrote the source?	....
What is the purpose of the source?	....
What is the main perspective on the issue?	....
What are its strengths?	....
What are its limitations?	....

What points do I agree with?	....
What points do I disagree with?	....

Peer feedback

Show your evaluation to a partner, and ask them to check the evaluation list and tell you:

Two things that they thought you identified clearly (write what they tell you here):

⭐ ....

⭐ ....

One thing that you could do better (write what they tell you here):

 ....

Class discussion

Do you agree?

Be ready to share your thinking.

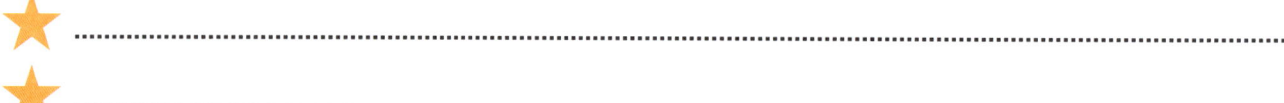

A one-sided source is never useful

Independent reflection activity

Check your learning goals

If you have achieved them and could teach someone else, put a '★'.

If you have achieved them independently, put a '☺'.

If you can achieve them with support, put a '☺'.

Developing evaluation skills: Lesson 4

| Lesson learning goals |

These are the goals for this lesson.
You will return to this table at the end of the lesson for the independent reflection activity.

My learning goals To develop my knowledge and understanding about:	I think	My teacher/ partner thinks
commenting on the strengths and limitations of a source		
identifying the perspective of a source and giving my own opinion on it		

What can I already do?

A good argument needs ....

....

....

How would you complete this sentence?

Starter activity

The group have made notes about different sources about an issue. Can you help them sort out their **opinions**? They need to know which ones are about the strengths of a source, which ones are about its limitations and which ones are about what perspective the source offers on the issue. The first one has been done for you.

Alice, Bird protection society

"I haven't visited the town, but know that seagulls will try to find food either out at sea or on land. Visitors to a seaside town that leave litter may be a source of food for the birds. Seagulls will only swoop down on food that they can see, so covering rubbish with a blanket will stop seagulls attacking rubbish to find food."

Jack, Environment officer

"Having looked at the wind patterns across the seaside town, I can see that the current bins are in the wrong place. Wind can be strong enough to lift rubbish out of full bins. There is a need to have stable bins in place that won't fall over in the wind and encouraging visitors to throw their rubbish in a bin."

Liz, Tourist

"I've heard about the issue with seagulls, but have never had a problem with them. I only visit as a tourist and just spend a few hours in the town. I don't really see what all the fuss is about!"

Mo, Town councillor

"I ordered new bins in to try and stop seagulls becoming a pest within our town. The bins I ordered are stable and stop seagulls trying to get into the rubbish."

Arun's notes

He is the person who decided to order new bins. He would not want to say that the bins were not effective if he ordered them.

Marcus's notes

She might not have been to the town, but she is an expert on seagull behaviour. She says a simple solution is to cover rubbish with a blanket.

Zara's notes

She does not spend a long time in the town. She has visited the town as a tourist. She doesn't see what the fuss is about.

Sofia's notes

He has said that the bins are in the wrong place because he has looked carefully into wind patterns. He might not have considered other explanations though.

Source	Strengths of the source	Limitations of the source	Perspectives on the issue in the source
Mo, Town councillor	He is the person who decided to order new bins so should know something about the design.	He would not want to say that the bins were not effective if he ordered them.	He thinks the **problem** will be sorted out.
	....	....	....
	....	....	He thinks the **problem** will be sorted out. ....
	....	....	....

Main activity

The issue I am focusing on today is:

....

Now it's your turn.

Your teacher will give you two sources. Look at them with your group. Read each source and consider its strengths and limitations. Identify the perspective each source gives and then reflect on your perspective. Write your evaluation in the table that follows the sources. You need to make sure you discuss how well you think each writer supports their perspective with evidence and reasoning. You will need to give your own judgement. Which points do you agree/disagree with? Why?

Use these phrases to help you. You will also need to use your own ideas.

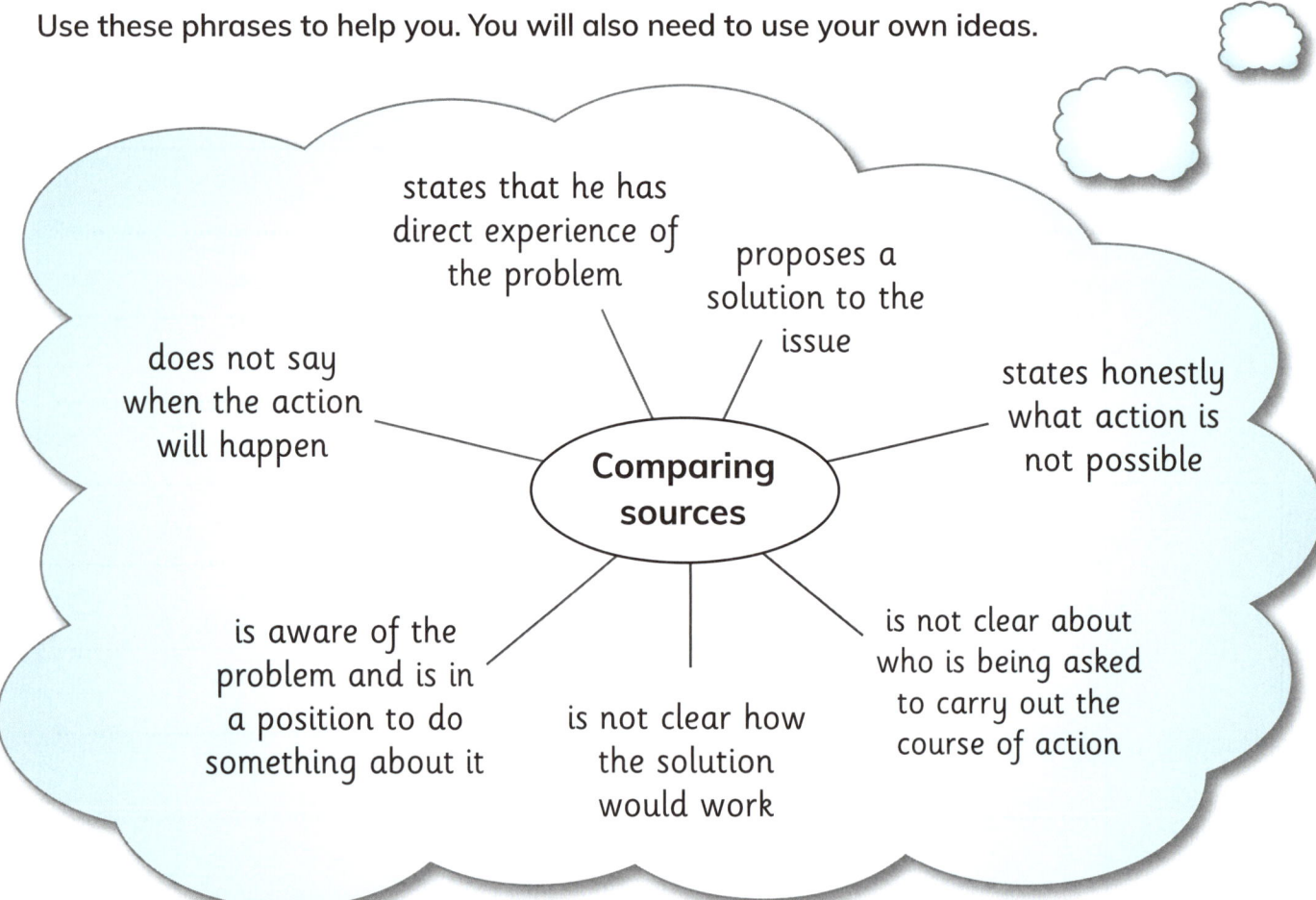

states that he has direct experience of the problem

proposes a solution to the issue

does not say when the action will happen

states honestly what action is not possible

Comparing sources

is aware of the problem and is in a position to do something about it

is not clear how the solution would work

is not clear about who is being asked to carry out the course of action

Class discussion

When someone is making an effective argument, they always …

When someone is making an effective argument, they never …

What do you think people always do when they set out a good argument?

What do you think people never do when they set out a good argument?

How would you finish Zara and Sofia's sentences?

Be ready to share your ideas.

Peer feedback

Show your evaluation to a partner from a different group, and ask them to tell you:

Two things that they like about your evaluation (write what they tell you here):

⭐ ....

⭐ ....

One thing that you could do better (write what they tell you here):

....

Independent reflection activity

Check your learning goals

If you have achieved them and could teach someone else, put a '★'.

If you have achieved them independently, put a '☺'.

If you can achieve them with support, put a '☹'.

Self-assessment Lessons 3–4

How will I know if I have achieved my learning goals?

Use this activity to reflect on how well you have progressed over the last two lessons.

Tick (✓) 'Achieved independently' if you feel confident that you could apply this skill for yourself.

Tick (✓) 'Achieved with support' if you still need some help when you apply this skill.

If you tick 'Achieved independently', then try to deepen your understanding and provide support for others when working on the next issue.

If you tick 'Achieved with support', look out for opportunities to consolidate this skill when working on the next issue.

Evaluation learning goals To develop my knowledge and understanding about:	Achieved independently	Achieved with support	I think this because
considering the author and purpose of a source			
identifying and commenting on the strengths and limitations of a source			
identifying the perspective of a source and giving my own opinion on it			

Issue review

Think about the issue you have been focusing on and complete the following statements.

I was surprised to discover/explore that ....

....

I did not know ....

....

I now think ....

....

Getting better at evaluation skills: Lesson 5

Lesson learning goals		
These are the goals for this lesson. You will return to this table at the end of the lesson for the independent reflection activity.		

My learning goals To get better at:	I think	My teacher/ partner thinks
discussing a source, its author and purpose, and its strengths and limitations		
saying what I think about someone else's perspective		

What can I already do?

Arun is doing some research about hunting. He finds these sources:

1 'Hunting Today' – a magazine for hunters
2 'Is hunting causing some animal species to go extinct?' – a scientific study of hunting
3 'Save our wildlife!' – a video made by animal lovers
4 'How hunting helps to save our forests' – a newspaper article
5 'My Life as a Hunter' – an autobiography
6 'Advice to Hunters' – a guide to staying safe when hunting

Write the number of each source in one of the squares in this grid:

	Trustworthy	Untrustworthy
For hunting		
Against hunting		

Talk with a partner. Why do you think some of these sources are more trustworthy than others?

Starter activity

Arun reads this headline in a national newspaper. Read the introduction to the newspaper article and then think about your answers to the questions for class discussion.

New law to create National Forest Parks
Ban on all hunting in parks

The government wants to pass a new law which will protect forests by turning them into National Parks, where hunting wildlife will be illegal.

Class discussion

1 What reasons could there be for this new law?
   Who would argue in favour of it and why?

2 What reasons could there be against the new law?
   Who would argue against it and why?

Main activity

The issue I am focusing on today is:

....

Read the sources that your teacher will give you (letters to the government about the new law) and work with your group to complete the top row of the table beneath it by filling columns A, B and C with a summary of what you find. Note down who makes the argument and whether they are for or against the new law, and give one reason or piece of evidence that they present to support this point of view (for or against).

Discuss each perspective in turn. Complete column D by summarising what members of your group think about the ideas in each source before you move on to discuss the next one.

Then work by yourself. Reflect on what you think about the points raised in the discussion. Summarise your own perspective on each argument in Column E.

Class discussion

1 Which argument do you agree with most?

2 Why do you agree with the argument? What was the most convincing?

Independent reflection activity

Check your learning goals

If you have achieved them and could teach someone else, put a '★'.

If you have achieved them independently, put a '☺'.

If you can achieve them with support, put a '☺'.

Self-assessment Lesson 5

How will I know if I have achieved my learning goals?

Use this activity to reflect on how well you have progressed over the last lesson.

Tick (✓) 'Achieved independently' if you feel confident that you could apply this skill for yourself.

Tick (✓) 'Achieved with support' if you still need some help when you apply this skill.

If you tick 'Achieved independently', then try to deepen your understanding and provide support for others when working on the next issue.

If you tick 'Achieved with support', look out for opportunities to consolidate this skill when working on the next issue.

Evaluation learning goals To get better at:	Achieved independently	Achieved with support	I think this because
discussing a source, its author and purpose and its strengths and limitations			
saying what I think about someone else's perspective			

Continued

Reflect on your responses in your self-assessment and identify one area for improvement.

One skill I want to get even better at is:

....

How I will improve:

....

Issue review

Think about the issue you have been focusing on and complete the following statements.

I was surprised to discover/explore that ....

....

I did not know ....

....

I now think ....

....

> Section 4
Reflection

In this section of your Learner's Skills Book you'll be developing your reflection skills while thinking about interesting issues.

But what does reflection involve?

How well do you work as a member of the team?

How can you help your team to achieve its goals? What do you do well as a member of the team, and what could you get better at?

How have your ideas changed as a result of learning new things about an issue?

What are the advantages and disadvantages of teamwork? How has teamwork helped you to learn new skills, or to improve existing skills?

Let's start thinking about reflection!

In Section 4: Reflection, you might choose to focus on the Challenge 'Where does all our packaging go?' and the topic 'Looking after planet Earth'.

If you take on this Challenge, you may be asked to keep a 'reflective log'. A reflective log is a place to record your reflections on teamwork and the activities you take part in. You'll use your log to record these things at each stage of the Challenge, not just at the end! By keeping a record like this, you'll be able to see how your attitudes and ideas change and develop during the Challenge.

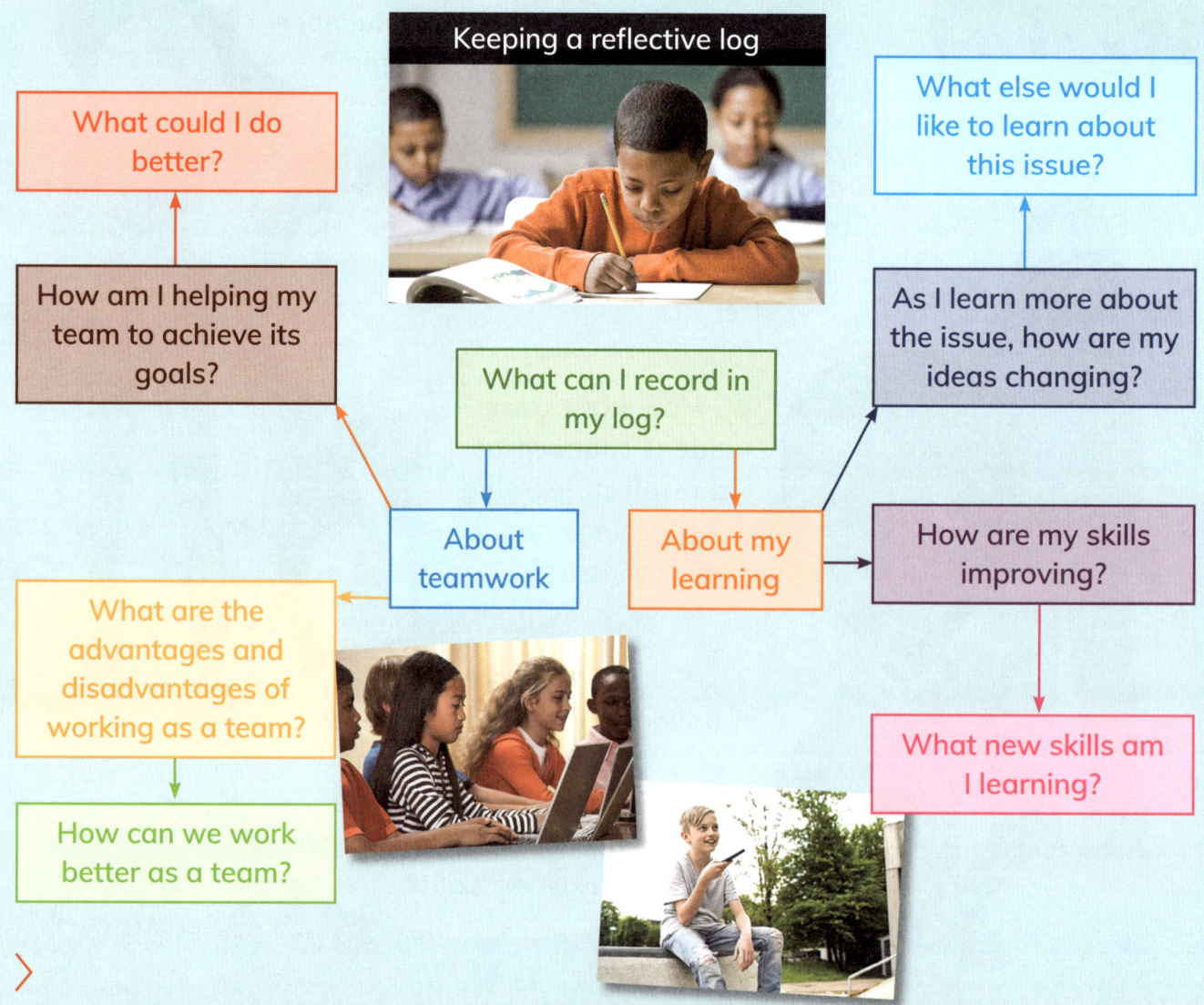

Keeping a reflective log

What could I do better?

What else would I like to learn about this issue?

How am I helping my team to achieve its goals?

As I learn more about the issue, how are my ideas changing?

What can I record in my log?

About teamwork

About my learning

How are my skills improving?

What are the advantages and disadvantages of working as a team?

How can we work better as a team?

What new skills am I learning?

Or you might choose to focus on the topics 'Digital world', 'Improving communication', 'Education for all' and 'Rich and poor', which you will look at in this section of your Learner's Skills Book.

Think about your answers to these questions:

- What are the things I do well to help my team achieve its goals?
  What can I get better at?

- What things are better when we work as a team? What things are more difficult?

- How have my ideas about an issue changed? Why have they changed?

- What has helped me to learn new skills, or improve the skills I already have?

Reflection words

attributes	depth	perspectives	resourcefulness
behaviour	fact	persuasive	responsibility
benefits	information	progress	role
challenges	learning goals	reasons	skills
confident	personal	research	source
contribution	contribution	resilience	teamwork

What is reflection?

Reflection: thinking about your experiences of working as a member of a team, and of taking part in learning activities

Reflection also includes:

- talking about what you do well as a team member, and what you could improve
- discussing positive and negative things about teamwork
- saying how your ideas about an issue have changed
- talking about the skills you've learned or improved by taking part in activities

Remember!

You can use any of the Challenges or topics as the starting point to develop your reflection skills. Your teacher may direct you to focus on a specific Challenge or topic, or you may be able to choose for yourself.

Starting with reflection skills: Lesson 1

In this chapter you will develop skills in reflection. In general, reflection means thinking about or considering something in depth. In Cambridge Primary Global Perspectives, reflection may involve thinking about how well you have achieved your learning goals, how your thinking about an issue or your behaviour has changed, how much progress you have made in developing your skills, etc. You may also be expected to reflect on your personal contribution to a team effort, and on the benefits and challenges of working as a team.

Lesson learning goals

These are the goals for this lesson.
You will return to this table at the end of the lesson for the independent reflection activity.

My learning goals To start to:	I think	My teacher/ partner thinks
talk about the benefits and challenges of working together towards a shared goal		
talk about what I have learned and how my ideas have changed		
talk about a skill that I have got better at		

What can I already do?

Sofia and her group were working on a presentation for worldwide Safer Internet Day in early February. Their goal was to make sure that children two years younger than them in their school understood how to stay safe online while doing their own research for Cambridge Primary Global Perspectives. The group was preparing a presentation.

Here are some of the things they said while they were working on their project.

Sofia: You should be careful what you believe about what you read online. Not all 'news' is true. People make things up.

Marcus: Apps sometimes can cost you money. You need to check with an adult about this.

Arun: Sometimes you get sent messages from people who want your passwords. That is called phishing.

Zara: Campaigners use social media to change people's ideas. It is age restricted.

Work in a group. If you were giving advice about internet safety to children two years younger than you, what would you say? How can they use the internet for their project and stay safe at the same time?

Write your ideas here.

1   ....

2   ....

3   ....

Tell the other members of your group the three pieces of advice you have written down, and explain why you chose them. Listen to the ideas that other members of your group tell you.

Starter activity

The issue I am focusing on today is:

....

These are some of the things that members of Zara's group said to each other after they had worked on their team presentation on internet safety.

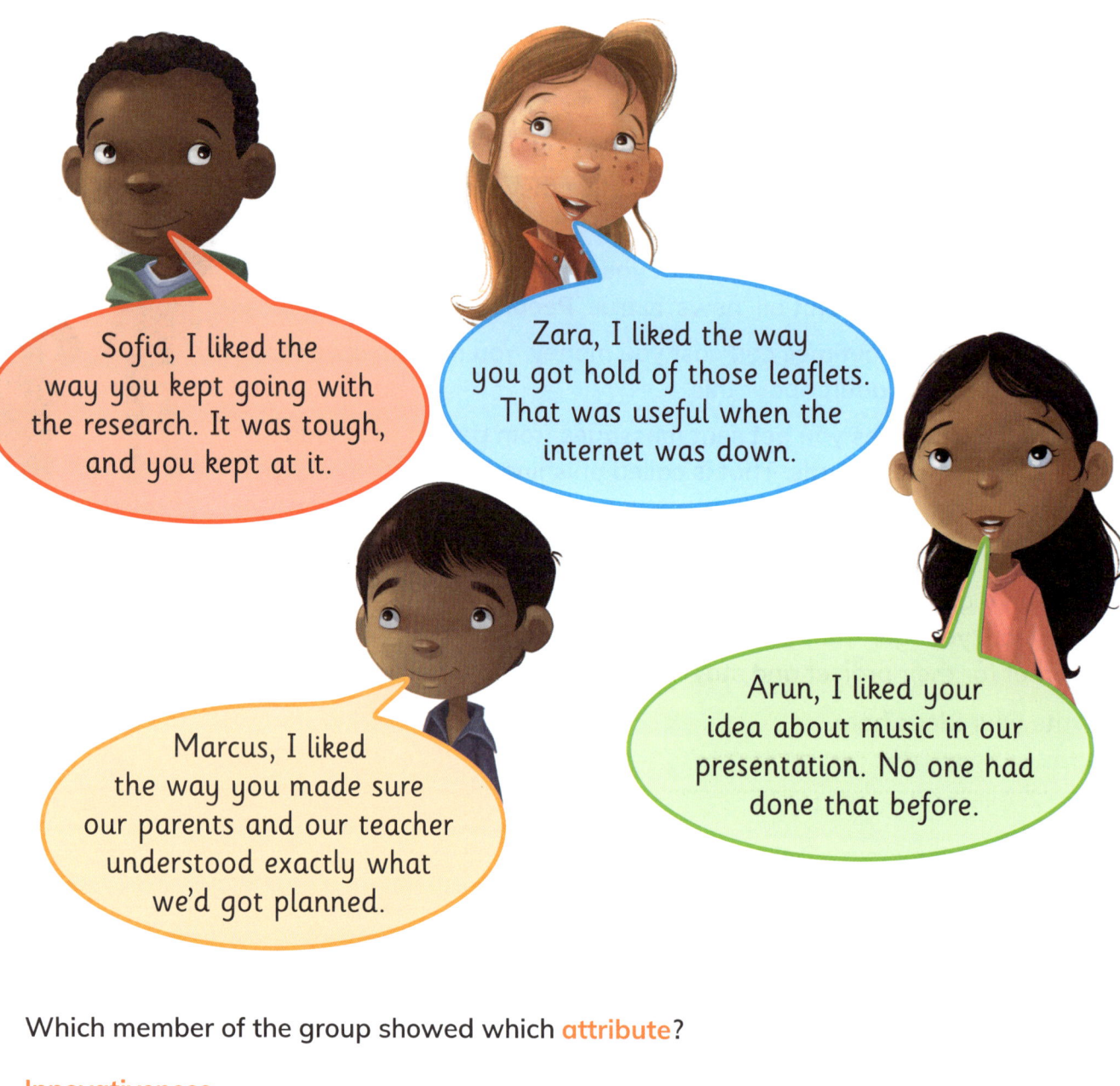

Sofia, I liked the way you kept going with the research. It was tough, and you kept at it.

Zara, I liked the way you got hold of those leaflets. That was useful when the internet was down.

Marcus, I liked the way you made sure our parents and our teacher understood exactly what we'd got planned.

Arun, I liked your idea about music in our presentation. No one had done that before.

Which member of the group showed which attribute?

Innovativeness ....

Responsibility ....

Resourcefulness ....

Resilience ....

Class discussion

1   What other attributes do you think effective team members have?

2   What attributes do you think you have developed so far that help you to be a good team member? What examples would you point to?

3   What attributes do you think you could work on so that you could contribute to teamwork even more effectively?

Main activity

Your teacher will give you and the members of your group a download containing information about e-safety. Some of it will be useful to you – some of it less so.

Imagine that your group are planning a presentation together based on this information. As a group, decide what you would tell children two years younger than you:

1   about the benefits of using the internet for their work on Cambridge Primary Global Perspectives

2   about the potential risks.

Now reflect on what you have learned and your individual contribution to the team effort.

1   Write down one important fact that you have learned about safety online.

    ....

2   Name one thing that you could do that would help younger children understand how to stay safe online.

    ....

3   How will today's learning affect what you do in the future?

    ....

4   What teamwork skills have you used in this activity?

    ....

Class discussion

How would you finish Arun's sentence?

You know you're in a good team when …

Independent reflection activity

Check your learning goals

If you have achieved them and could teach someone else, put a '★'.

If you have achieved them independently, put a '☺'.

If you can achieve them with support, put a '☺'.

2

Starting with reflection skills: Lesson 2

Lesson learning goals		
These are the goals for this lesson. You will return to this table at the end of the lesson for the independent reflection activity.		
My learning goals To start to:	I think	My teacher/ partner thinks
talk about what I did as a member of my team		
talk about the benefits and challenges of working as a member of a team		

What can I already do?

Arun uses the internet regularly. He recently found this source:

> Many 8 to 12 year olds use social media and enjoy sharing fun ideas with friends, keeping in touch with relatives and for finding information. What's wrong with that? The **problem** is, it is simply not safe for children to use social media without the right controls. Companies should enforce the age limits for their apps – but they don't. There is too much material online that is not suitable for young people. And what are the **consequences**? A growing number of **psychiatrists** say young people are suffering. They see material designed for adults. They miss out on sleep.

1   Who do you think wrote this? (Tick one)

a   A computer repair company ☐

b   An internet-safety campaigner ☐

c   An advertiser for a tech company ☐

d   A scientist studying the human brain ☐

2   Why do you think they wrote it? (Tick one)

a   To report on how the brain works ☐

b   To sell more computers ☐

c   To advise people to check their internet connection ☐

d   To persuade people to be more careful online ☐

Discuss the following questions with a partner.

1   What do you use the internet for?
2   What action do you think Arun could take after reading this?

Starter activity

The issue I am focusing on today is:

....

Arun and his group asked children in their year group for reasons why people go online. They made a list.

What are the potential risks?

Number them from 1–10, with 1 being the one you think is most risky and 10 the one you think is least risky.

Reason for going online	Risk factor (1–10)
To research for homework	
To play games online	
To contact learners in partner schools	
To send emails	
To find out what is happening in the world	
To check on social media	
To find out about their favourite sports team	
To watch live streams of events	
To find out about their favourite artists	
To share their creative ideas with others	

Talk to a partner about when you go online and why.

What could someone your age do if they were worried about something that took place online?

Class discussion

Studies have found that young people who check their social media more than three times a day are less happy as a result. Many miss out on exercise and sleep.

1   What happens when people your age spend too much time online?

2   What are the risks of being online?

3   What can be done to reduce these risks?

Main activity

Sofia and her group have been talking about ways in which they could help persuade people in their year group to reduce the amount of time they spend in front of a screen. They want to give them positive alternatives.

Search engines can turn up many different **perspectives**; but you can find different ones again in the library.

Instead of playing an online cricket game, you could actually go out and play cricket!

You don't need to know what everyone else is up to all of the time. It is nice just to take time to chill out.

When my uncle doesn't want to be bothered by anyone, he puts his phone in the bathroom cabinet!

Work in a group. Before you begin this activity, decide if there is a specific role each member of the team would like to take? Look at the list of reasons for being in front of a screen in the Starter activity. With the other members of your group, choose four of them that you would all like to help reduce. What action could you take?

Reasons for being in front of a screen	Positive alternative

Peer feedback

Think about the activity you have just done in your group. For each person in your group, including yourself, think of one way that they helped the group to complete this activity.

Name of group member	Contribution to teamwork

Share your ideas with the others in your group, and decide what the most helpful thing that each person did was.

1   What do the other group members think your most helpful contribution was? Write it here:

....

2   What was one advantage of doing this activity as a team?

....

3   What was one difficulty to overcome?

....

Class discussion

1   What are the different ways that each group member can help to make teamwork successful?
2   How can your teamwork be improved?

Independent reflection activity

Check your learning goals

If you have achieved them and could teach someone else, put a '★'.

If you have achieved them independently, put a '☺'.

If you can achieve them with support, put a '☺'.

3

Starting with reflection skills: Lesson 3

Lesson learning goals		
These are the goals for this lesson. You will return to this table at the end of the lesson for the independent reflection activity.		
My learning goals **To start to:**	I think	My teacher/ partner thinks
talk about what I did as a member of my team		
talk about the benefits and challenges of working as a member of a team		
talk about what I have learned and how my ideas have changed		
talk about a skill that I have got better at		

What can I already do?

Here are some of the things that Sofia's group said when they reflected on their team project.

Sofia: What I did positively for the team was keeping going with the research. I need to get better at understanding different perspectives in the group.

Zara: I learned a lot about how tech companies use information about what you do online to make money. I used to think everyone saw the same adverts. I now know it is much more complex.

Arun: There is no way we would have been able to include great music in our **presentation** if we hadn't been in a team. It was difficult to get everyone to agree, though.

Marcus: I am definitely going to monitor my screen time, especially in the evening. There's an app that does this for you.

Talk to a partner.

Choice A: Tell them about what you have done positively for the team and what you want to develop. Sofia did this.

Choice B: Tell them about the plus points and difficulties you have found so far working as part of a team. Arun did this.

Choice C: Tell them about how your understanding of the issue has developed. Zara did this.

Choice D: Tell them about something you are going to do differently because of what you have found out. Marcus did this.

Which aspects of teamwork do you feel **confident** in? Which would you like to improve at?

First activity

The issue I am focusing on today is:

....

Sofia and her group have been given permission to record a 'Public Information Broadcast', which can be played over the school's loudspeaker system, to persuade them to limit their daily screen time. They want to explain their message but time is limited: they only have 15 seconds to get their message across.

Imagine you and your group are in a similar situation to Sofia's group. Work with the other group members to plan and perform this. (At this stage, you only need to do a 'first take' – you can rehearse and improve your broadcast later.)

Use A4 paper or your preferred material to write down ideas.

Things to think about:

- What is your key message?
- What persuasive techniques will you use?
- How can you best organise the work among the members of your team?

Second activity

With a partner, reflect on the teamwork activity that your group has just done.

	Me	My partner
Something good about the way your team worked		
Something that could be improved next time		
Something you learned about teamwork		
Something you did that helped your team		
Something you could do differently next time		
Some skills that you used during teamwork		

Report back to the class. What was similar about you and your partner's experiences during the teamwork activity? What was different?

Class discussion

1 How did your group make sure that everyone took part effectively?
2 How did your group make sure that the work was finished on time?
3 If you could work together on this task again, what would you improve? How?

Independent reflection activity

Check your learning goals

If you have achieved them and could teach someone else, put a '★'.

If you have achieved them independently, put a '☺'.

If you can achieve them with support, put a '☺'.

Self-assessment Lessons 1–3

How will I know if I have achieved my learning goals?

Use this activity to reflect on how well you have progressed over the last three lessons.

Tick (✓) 'Achieved independently' if you feel confident that you could apply this skill for yourself.

Tick (✓) 'Achieved with support' if you still need some help when you apply this skill.

If you tick 'Achieved independently', then try to deepen your understanding and provide support for others when working on the next issue.

If you tick 'Achieved with support', look out for opportunities to consolidate this skill when working on the next issue.

Reflection learning goals To start to:	Achieved independently	Achieved with support	I think this because
talk about what I did as a member of my team			
talk about the benefits and challenges of working as a member of a team towards a shared goal			
talk about what I have learned and how my ideas have changed			
talk about a skill that I have got better at			

Issue review

Think about the issue you have been focusing on and complete the following statements.

I was surprised to discover/explore that ....

....

I did not know ....

....

I now think ....

....

Developing reflection skills: Lesson 4

Lesson learning goals		
These are the goals for this lesson. You will return to this table at the end of the lesson for the independent reflection activity.		
My learning goals **To develop my knowledge and understanding about:**	I think	My teacher/ partner thinks
how to talk about what I did as a member of my team		
how to talk about the benefits and challenges of working as a member of a team		

What can I already do?

Look at the texts about using the internet below, and match each text with a source. One example has been done for you.

Sources

A   Advertisement for antivirus software

B   Business Studies textbook

C   Newspaper article

D   Post on an online technology blog

E   Video posted online

Texts

1   According to a recent industry report, ransomware attacks are rising sharply. In some countries, it is estimated that they hit businesses up to 50 percent more than just 6 months ago. | C |

2   Our safety-conscious users value the browsing security our multiple layer systems bring. For best results, get Centurion. | |

3   Has anyone else noticed how slow the bandwidth is getting today? Normally I can download my jpeg files straight away, but today everything just keeps timing out. I'm so frustrated! | |

4   When I got my first home computer, if I wanted to go online, I would use dial-up. You used to get excited if you got an email! Now look at this nonsense; my notification is showing over 14,000! | |

5   Cookies are an important part of the business model. Many tech companies depend on cookies as a source of income, without which they could not survive. | |

Talk to a partner. Which sources do you think give the most reliable information about how the internet works? Why?

Class discussion

1   What do you know about cyber threats?

2   How does knowing about cyber threats affect how you behave online?

First activity

The issue I am focusing on today is:

....

Marcus, Sofia, Arun and Zara are working on a team project about staying safe online. They want to raise people's awareness about the importance of e-safety, and have thought of four questions to do research on. Each of them has made notes from a different source, and now they are going to share information in order to complete this grid.

E-safety project	
What can I trust online?	How do I check if an app or website is safe to use?
How do I create a good password?	How can I keep my account private?

Work in a group. Your teacher will give each of you a different set of notes about e-safety and a template so that you can complete the grid. Share the information with others in your group by telling them anything from your notes that will help to answer the questions. Write down information that the others tell you in the appropriate boxes. (Tip: you will only have a limited time to do this and you may not need all the information in your notes. Share the information that you think is most important with your group.)

Second activity

Reflect on the previous activity and think about your answers to these questions. Then discuss them with a partner:

1 How did you help your group to complete the task?

....

....

2 What could you have done better or differently to help your group complete the task more efficiently or more effectively?

....

....

3 In what ways did working as a team make it easier to complete the task?

....

....

4 Are there any ways that working as a team make it more challenging to complete the task?

....

....

Class discussion

1 What are the advantages of working as a team?
2 What are the challenges of working as a team?
3 How can an individual member of a team best help the whole team to reach their goal?
4 How can a team best help an individual to contribute?

Independent reflection activity

Check your learning goals

If you have achieved them and could teach someone else, put a '★'.

If you have achieved them independently, put a '☺'.

If you can achieve them with support, put a '☺'.

Developing reflection skills: Lesson 5

Lesson learning goals		
These are the goals for this lesson. You will return to this table at the end of the lesson for the independent reflection activity.		
My learning goals To develop my knowledge and understanding about:	I think	My teacher/ partner thinks
how to talk about what I have learned and how my ideas have changed		
how to talk about a skill that I have got better at		

What can I already do?

Arun is reflecting on a teamwork activity he took part in.
Read what he says and think about the answers to the questions.

Before my team did some research on e-safety, I used to think that the only problem with information online was that there was just so much of it. Then one of the members of my team told me that false stories get put online as '**click bait**'. I looked online and found an article that explained about **terms and conditions**. You can end up agreeing to sharing your location or even your camera if you aren't careful. I've learned always to check before I click 'agree'. So I suggested to my team that we could record a **podcast** for the school shared area and they agreed.

1   What facts has Arun learned about e-safety?
2   How has this changed the way he thinks about information online?
3   What did Arun contribute to his team?
4   What skills did Arun use during the teamwork activity?

Talk with a partner. Discuss the answers to the questions.

Starter activity

The issue I am focusing on today is:

....

Marcus, Sofia, Arun and Zara have made a group decision to create a podcast to raise other children's awareness of fake news. The school's IT coordinator has agreed to check and upload the recording to the shared area when it is good enough. It can then be accessed by each class.

Class discussion

1 What makes a good podcast?

2 What information about fake news do you think the team should include in their podcast?

3 Why do you think they need to include this information?

4 The team discuss what tasks they will need to complete in order to create their podcast. Read their list of tasks in the download that your teacher will give you. The team have not yet decided who should do each task, how they should do it and how long each should take. Thy have only completed the first row in the table. What do you think the other members of the team could be doing while Arun performs task 1? What tasks do you think could be done best by individuals? What tasks do you think could be done best by the whole team working together? Help the team plan their project by completing the other rows of the table. They were only given three hours to complete the whole project.

Main activity

Work in a group. Now plan how your group would carry out the fake news podcast project. Think about the tasks that need to be done, and decide:

- What tasks will you do in your group?
- Who in your team will do each of the tasks
- How will they do it?
- In what order and for how long will they do it?

Complete the table.

Make sure you know how long you will have to finish the project. This will help you decide how long to spend on each task.

Class discussion

1 What challenges did you face when working as a team to complete the plan, and how did you overcome them?

2 What skills did you use?

3 What skills would you like to get better at?

4 If you were going to do this activity again, how could you do things differently?

Peer feedback

Show your completed team plan to someone from a different group, and ask them to tell you the answers to these questions:

1   Will each member of the team be equally challenged in the tasks?   YES/NO/MAYBE
2   Has the team chosen the most efficient or effective way
    for Arun's team to complete each of the tasks?   YES/NO/MAYBE
3   Can the project be completed in the time available?   YES/NO/MAYBE

If the answer to any of the questions is 'NO', what changes could be made to the plan?

....

....

Independent reflection activity

Check your learning goals

If you have achieved them and could teach someone else, put a '★'.

If you have achieved them independently, put a '☺'.

If you can achieve them with support, put a '☺'.

Developing reflection skills: Lesson 6

Lesson learning goals

These are the goals for this lesson.
You will return to this table at the end of the lesson for the independent reflection activity.

My learning goals To develop my knowledge and understanding about:	I think	My teacher/ partner thinks
how to talk about what I did as a member of my team		
how to talk about the benefits and challenges of working as a member of a team		
how to talk about what I have learned and how my ideas have changed		
how to talk about a skill that I have got better at		

What can I already do?

Sofia has been reflecting on a project that her team has completed recently. She writes a personal reflection, which includes a number of different topics. Match the topics to the numbers in the text. An example has been done for you.

Topic	Number(s)	Personal reflection
a How working as a team helped Sofia.		**(1)** Our team decided to make a podcast full of e-safety tips for the **shared drive**. **(2)** One of my jobs was to create a memorable slogan about e-safety. I volunteered to do this because I wanted to develop my innovation skills. **(3)** The slogan was not as simple as I wanted. The team gave me a lot of ideas to put in and it took time for me to come to a decision. **(4)** This was because each member of our team wanted their ideas included, **(5)** so I decided to put the ideas together in a mind map. **(6)** Luckily, another member of the team helped me choose between my three final ideas, so we were still able to finish the work in time for the ICT coordinator's **deadline**. **(7)** From this experience, I learned that it would be useful to have some space to consider what the others have said and to make sure that I report back when I have finished my task. When it was time for other classes to access our podcast, I felt very nervous about **(8)** whether my voice was expressive for the listeners, but **(9)** the other team members had helped me try out different ways to say my sections in front of the microphone. In the end, the teachers and children told us our team's podcast was fun and had great ideas!
b What the team's goal was.	(1)	
c What Sofia did to help the team achieve its goal.		
d Something Sofia thinks would make teamwork better in future.		
e What Sofia thinks of her efforts to help the team.		
f What Sofia found challenging about working in a team.		

First activity

The issue I am focusing on today is:

....

Work in a group. Look at the plan for the podcast that your team made in Lesson 5. Record your podcast with the other members of your group.

Second activity

1 Think about how you worked as a member of a team. Make a note of:

a One thing that you personally did to help the team achieve its goal.

....

b One thing that you would do differently in future.

....

2 Think about the way your team worked. Make a note of:

a One thing your team did that worked well.

....

b One thing that could be improved to make your teamwork even better next time.

....

3 Think about how your ideas about teamwork have changed over the past three lessons. Complete this sentence:

I used to think ....

....

but now I think ....

....

4   Think about one thing that has changed in the way you do teamwork.
    Complete this sentence:

    In the past, when I worked in a team, I used to ....

    ....

    but now I ....

    ....

Class discussion

1   What have you learned about being a member of a team?
2   How can teamwork be improved?

Independent reflection activity

Check your learning goals

If you have achieved them and could teach someone else, put a '★'.

If you have achieved them independently, put a '☺'.

If you can achieve them with support, put a '☺'.

Self-assessment Lessons 4–6

How will I know if I have achieved my learning goals?

Use this activity to reflect on how well you have progressed over the last three lessons.

Tick (✓) 'Achieved independently' if you feel confident that you could apply this skill for yourself.

Tick (✓) 'Achieved with support' if you still need some help when you apply this skill.

If you tick 'Achieved independently', then try to deepen your understanding and provide support for others when working on the next issue.

If you tick 'Achieved with support', look out for opportunities to consolidate this skill when working on the next issue.

Reflection learning goals To develop my knowledge and understanding about:	Achieved independently	Achieved with support	I think this because
how to talk about what I did as a member of my team			
how to talk about the benefits and challenges of working as a member of a team			
how to talk about what I have learned and how my ideas have changed			
how to talk about a skill that I have got better at			

Issue review

Think about the issue you have been focusing on and complete the following statements.

I was surprised to discover/explore that ....

....

I did not know ....

....

I now think ....

....

Within the image on the whiteboard:
How many sides?
What shape are the sides?
How many edges?
How many vertices?
Is it a polyhedron?
Where might you see this shape?

Getting better at reflection skills: Lesson 7

Lesson learning goals		
These are the goals for this lesson. You will return to this table at the end of the lesson for the independent reflection activity.		
My learning goals To get better at:	I think	My teacher/ partner thinks
talking about what I have learned and how my ideas have changed		
talking about a skill that I have got better at		

What can I already do?

Zara is thinking about what it is like to be a child in her country. She chooses a colour, a symbol and an image to represent being a child. Zara explains her ideas:

'I chose the colour green because a child is like a plant growing. I chose a nest as a symbol because children need to grow in a safe place. I drew an image of a child walking along a path because children are beginning a journey to the future.'

Think about what it is like to be a child in your country.
Choose a colour, a symbol and an image. Draw them here:

Being a child is like . . .

Colour

Symbol

Image

Talk with a partner. Share your ideas about what it is like to be a child in your country.

Starter activity

Zara and her classmates are doing a project about primary school education around the world. They have come up with four questions that they want to find answers to. Read their questions, and then think about your answers to the questions for class discussion.

Class discussion

1   What do you think the answers to these questions are?
2   How could you find out more?

Main activity

The issue I am focusing on today is:

....

Work in a group. Share the information that your teacher gives you, so that you find at least two answers to each of the questions that Zara and her classmates ask.

Tell a partner your answers to these questions.

1   From doing this activity, what have you learned about:

   a   Children's education around the world?

   b   Working as a member of a team?

2   How has this changed your ideas about:

   a   Children's education?

   b   Teamwork?

3   During this activity:

   a   What skills did you use?

   b   What skill did you get better at?

Independent reflection activity

Check your learning goals

If you have achieved them and could teach someone else, put a '★'.

If you have achieved them independently, put a '☺'.

If you can achieve them with support, put a '☺'.

Getting better at reflection skills: Lesson 8

Lesson learning goals		
These are the goals for this lesson. You will return to this table at the end of the lesson for the independent reflection activity.		
My learning goals To get better at:	I think	My teacher/ partner thinks
talking about what I did as a member of my team		
talking about the benefits and challenges of working as a member of a team		

What can I already do?

Here is a list of some roles that can help a group to work together as a team, with a description of what each role involves.

Role	Description	Answers question
Timekeeper	Checks that the group completes the task within the deadline.	
Scribe	Records the group's work by writing things down and keeping notes.	
Resource manager	Helps the group to find all the things they need to complete the task.	A
Presenter	Reports to the rest of the class about what the group has done.	
Facilitator	Makes sure that everyone has the chance to speak and make a contribution.	
Checker	Looks at the group's work to check that it achieves the goal and is free of errors.	

Who answers each of these questions? One example has been done for you.

A 'Are there any scissors to cut this paper with?'	B 'Have we done everything we're supposed to do?'	C 'How much longer have we got?'
D 'Is there anyone who hasn't spoken yet?'	E 'What are you going to tell them about our work?'	F 'What was the second thing we decided to do?'

Talk with a partner.
Which of these roles do you prefer when you do teamwork? Why?

Starter activity

Zara and her classmates want to make more people aware of the fact that many children around the world do not have a proper primary school education. They decide to write a short dramatic **sketch** to show why some children don't go to primary school. Read what they've written so far, and think about your answers to the questions for the class discussion.

Title: School is for everyone

Scene:
A father, mother and their daughter are at home. There is a knock at the door. The father opens the door. A support worker from the local primary school is outside.

Father (grumpily): Yes, can I help you?

Support worker: I've come to ask why your daughter isn't attending school. She's old enough, and I can see that she isn't ill. So why isn't she at school?

Class discussion

1 What could be the reason why the daughter is not attending primary school?
2 How could the support worker persuade the parents to let their daughter attend school?

Main activity

The issue I am focusing on today is:

....

Zara's group has written some more of their sketch, but there are some gaps.
Decide in your group how you think Zara's sketch should be completed.

Father: My wife's been ill for a long time, and so our daughter's been helping her to do all the housework.

Support worker:

Mother: It's true that our daughter has been very helpful, but I want her to have a good education, so that she can do more with her life.

Support worker:

Father:

Support worker: What does your daughter think?
Daughter:

Peer feedback

Now tell a partner your answers to these questions:

- What did you do to help your group complete the task in the Main activity?
- How do you feel about what you did?
- What skills did you use?
- Which of these skills do you think you are getting better at?
- What did you learn about teamwork from this activity?
- What would you like to change next time?

Ask your partner to note down:

Two positive things about your work as a member of a team during this activity (write what they tell you here):

⭐ ....

⭐ ....

One thing that you could do better (write what they tell you here):

 ....

Independent reflection activity

Check your learning goals

If you have achieved them and could teach someone else, put a '★'.

If you have achieved them independently, put a '☺'.

If you can achieve them with support, put a '☹'.

9

Getting better at reflection skills: Lesson 9

What can I already do?

Arun is thinking of words that are connected with the idea of teamwork. He says:

> I think the most important word is 'together' because that describes how we should work as a team.

What words come to your mind when you think about teamwork? Think of up to ten words, and write them on a sheet of paper in a word cloud, like the one below. You can write your words anywhere in the cloud, but remember: the more important a word is, the BIGGER it should be!

Talk with a partner. Explain why you chose these words to put in your word cloud.

Starter activity

As part of a presentation to their class, Zara's group members are going to create two tableaux vivants to show the contrast between children who receive a primary education and those who do not.

In your group, plan two tableaux like Zara's. Every member of your group should appear in both tableaux. Decide who each group member will represent in the tableaux and what **props** you might need. On a separate sheet of paper, draw or write what each of your tableaux will show:

Perform your tableaux to the rest of the class.

Main activity

The issue I am focusing on today is:

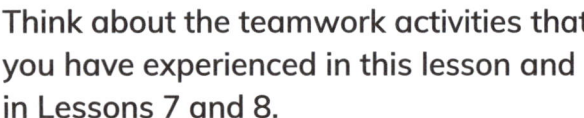

Think about the teamwork activities that you have experienced in this lesson and in Lessons 7 and 8.

1 Think of one example of something that went well for you and your group.

Tell a partner:

a What happened?

b Why do you think it happened?

c How could you make sure it happens again?

2 Think of one example of something that didn't go so well for you and your group.

Tell a partner:

a What happened?

b Why do you think it happened?

c How could you make it better in the future?

Class discussion

1 How have your ideas about teamwork changed?

2 What experiences (positive and negative) have helped you to change your ideas about teamwork?

Independent reflection activity

Check your learning goals

If you have achieved them and could teach someone else, put a '★'.

If you have achieved them independently, put a '☺'.

If you can achieve them with support, put a '☺'.

Self-assessment Lessons 7–9

How will I know if I have achieved my learning goals?

Use this activity to reflect on how well you have progressed over the last three lessons.

Tick (✓) 'Achieved independently' if you feel confident that you could apply this skill for yourself.

Tick (✓) 'Achieved with support' if you still need some help when you apply this skill.

If you tick 'Achieved independently', then try to deepen your understanding and provide support for others when working on the next issue.

If you tick 'Achieved with support', look out for opportunities to consolidate this skill when working on the next issue.

Reflection learning goals To get better at:	Achieved independently	Achieved with support	I think this because
talking about what I did as a member of my team			
talking about the benefits and challenges of working as a member of a team			
talking about what I have learned and how my ideas have changed			

Continued

Reflection learning goals To get better at:	Achieved independently	Achieved with support	I think this because
talking about a skill that I have got better at			

Reflect on your responses in your self-assessment and identify one area for improvement.

One skill I want to get even better at is:

....

How I will improve:

....

Issue review

Think about the issue you have been focusing on and complete the following statements.

I was surprised to discover/explore that ....

....

I did not know ....

....

I now think ....

....

Collaboration

In this section of your Learner's Skills Book you'll be developing your collaboration skills while thinking about interesting global issues.

But what does collaboration involve?

Do you share ideas with the rest of your team about how you can achieve the goal? Do you listen when others share their ideas?

How do your team plan work together so that each member knows what they should do, and everyone does their fair share of the work? When there are problems, how do you find ways of reaching an agreement?

Does every team member have the chance to speak so that the team finds the best way to work towards the goal?

How do you identify tasks for each individual to do that match their skills? How can you make sure that all tasks are completed on time?

Let's start thinking about collaboration!

In Section 5: Collaboration, you might choose to focus on the Challenge 'Will a robot do your job?' and the topic 'The world of work'.

If you take on this Challenge, you and your team will work together to prepare a radio broadcast or podcast. Here are some questions you and your team members can ask when deciding how to do this.

What are the other team members' ideas?

Give others the chance to speak, and listen to their ideas

Your team's goal (Preparing a radio broadcast or podcast)

What are my ideas about how to do this?

Share your ideas with the rest of the team

What do we do if there are disagreements?

Work together to solve problems

Make sure that each member of the team does something that they are good at

How do we plan to do the work?

Divide the work into separate tasks and share them equally, so everyone has something to do

Think about how long each task will take, so that the work is finished on time

Or you might choose to focus on the topics 'Education for all' and 'Health and wellbeing', which you will look at in this section of your Learner's Skills Book.

Think about your answers to these questions:

- What is our team's goal, and how do I think can we achieve it?
- What ideas do other team members have about how to achieve our goal?
- If there are problems, how can we work together to solve them?
- What can each member of the team do best to help us achieve our goal?
- Are there ways we could work better as a team?

Collaboration words

agreement	evaluate	perspective	responsible
attributes	facts	positive suggestions	shared outcome
effectively	innovative	reason	skills
encouraged	opinion	research	teamwork

What is collaboration?

Collaboration: working as part of a team to achieve a goal

Collaboration also includes:

- sharing ideas with your team, and listening to others
- working together to solve any problems that your team faces
- as a team, planning the best way to achieve your goal

Remember!

You can use any of the Challenges or topics as the starting point to develop your collaboration skills. Your teacher may direct you to focus on a specific Challenge or topic, or you may be able to choose for yourself.

Starting with collaboration skills: Lesson 1

In this chapter you will develop skills in collaboration. Collaboration means working together with other people to achieve a shared outcome or to resolve an issue. Remember, an issue is an important subject or problem for discussion.

Lesson learning goals

These are the goals for this lesson.
You will return to this table at the end of the lesson for the independent reflection activity.

My learning goals To start to:	I think	My teacher/ partner thinks
contribute useful ideas in my team		
help my team to solve problems		
help my team to plan tasks		
respect other team members' ideas about how to reach a goal		

What can I already do?

Arun is reflecting on how his perspective has changed as a result of some research his group carried out into child labour. Read his reflection below.

> Before we started our research on child labour, ==I thought that it was just== something ==from History==. But then I read that children work long hours making things we buy – like footballs and mobile phones. This made me realise that this is a serious issue and we will only find a solution if people start asking some serious questions. So I am going to ask on the company's website if they know for sure that no children worked on their product.

Now read the questions below, and highlight the text in Arun's reflection that matches each question, using the colour shown. One has been done for you.

Question	Colour
What did he think about child labour at first?	(pink)
What did he learn?	(yellow)
What does he think about it now?	(green)
What does he do differently now?	(blue)

Think of a global issue that you became aware of. What did you think before you studied it? How did your ideas change? Talk with a partner.

Starter activity

The issue I am focusing on today is:

....

The United Nations day of action against child labour is on 12 June. Arun and his group wanted to raise awareness about the problems faced by children who do not go to school because they have to work to support their families.

To prepare for their day of action, Arun's group decided to put on an assembly with a theatre performance. They thought of tasks that they would need to perform in order for it to be successful.

Can you think of anything to add to their list?

We need accurate **facts**. Who could we ask? We'll need to write the script this week.

Good thinking, Sofia. How about **UNICEF**? Maybe we should do a scene plan first.

I like the scene plan idea. We should practise moves as well as words. Where can we work?

Let me check ... The small hall is free on Tuesday at 11.15 a.m. and Thursday at 2.30 p.m.

Class discussion

1   When have you had to work together as part of a group on a task that had a **deadline**?

2   What was the end goal of your task?

3   What order did you do things in?

4   How well did your group make sure you met your deadline?

5   How well did your group make sure everyone contributed **effectively**?

6   How well did your group help each member of the team to develop their **skills**?

Main activity

Arun's group decided to put on a performance in a school assembly.
The group had four weeks in which to prepare their assembly.
They also wanted to invite a guest speaker from UNICEF.

Read their action plan in the download that your teacher will give you.

1   Have they planned to do things in the right order?

2   How well do you think they have planned to use the time?

3   How well do you think they have planned their use of the group members?

With your group, revise the plan, making any changes you think necessary
using the download that your teacher will give you.

Class discussion

What changes have you made to the original plan? Why?

Independent reflection activity

Check your learning goals

If you have achieved them and could teach someone else, put a '★'.

If you have achieved them independently, put a '☺'.

If you can achieve them with support, put a '☺'.

2

Starting with collaboration skills: Lesson 2

Lesson learning goals		
These are the goals for this lesson. You will return to this table at the end of the lesson for the independent reflection activity.		
My learning goals **To start to:**	I think	My teacher/ partner thinks
contribute useful ideas in my team		
help my team to solve problems		
help my team to plan tasks		
respect other team members' ideas about how to reach a goal		

What can I already do?

The team are talking about what attributes they saw in each other's work when they put on the performance for the 12 June day of action on child labour.

Arun: Sofia, I really like the way that you clearly explained to us why child labour is against children's human rights.

Sofia: Marcus, you were able to take a step back. You asked, 'What have we learned from the examples of child labour we looked at earlier?'

Marcus: Zara, the drumming idea you had for the performance to show the sound of the machinery was brilliant. No one had thought of using sound like that.

Zara: Arun, the chart with the list we could tick off was your idea. It really helped us make sure we got everything done on time.

Can you finish these sentences? Choose one of the following four attributes: confident, responsible, reflective, innovative. The first one has been done for you.

1   Arun talked about the way that Sofia was ......confident..

2   Sofia talked about the way that Marcus was ....

3   Marcus talked about the way that Zara was ....

4   Zara talked about the way that Arun was ....

Talk to a partner. Pick one of these attributes. Tell your partner about a time when you have seen one of them used in a group activity. What attribute was it? What difference did it make to the outcome?

Starter activity

The issue I am focusing on today is:

Work in a group. Imagine that your group is going to put on a performance to raise other learners' awareness about a United Nations day of action on an issue.

Here are your choices:

Date	Action	Reason
20 Feb	World Day of Social Justice	To make the world a fairer place for all its people.
22 March	World Water Day	To highlight the importance of making sure that everyone has access to clean water.
22 April	Mother Earth Day	To highlight the need to protect nature.
21 September	International Day of Peace	To highlight the need to build a peaceful world where people and nations work together.

On [insert date] ...., we are marking [insert action] ....

in order to [insert reason] ....

What tasks will your group need to do to prepare your performance? Make a list.
What skills will your group need to develop to put on an effective performance? Make a list.

Main activity

Imagine that you have four weeks to get everything ready for your performance, which has to take place on the day of action. Working in your group, complete the work plan. Your teacher will give you a download to help with this.

Report back to the class on your planning process.

Class discussion

1   What roles did each of your group members have while doing these activities?
2   What skills did you have already that enabled you to complete your plan?
3   What skills could you improve on so that you could work even better as a team?
4   How successful do you think your planning has been? How could it be improved?
5   Did your group have any different perspectives on the best way forward?
    If so, how did you form a single plan?
6   What changed about the way you worked as a team in Lesson 2 compared
    to Lesson 1?

Peer feedback

Talk to a partner from a different group about what you did in this lesson.
Tell your partner about the following:

1   A problem that your group encountered and how you dealt with it.
2   A helpful idea that you came up with.
3   An idea that another member of the group suggested and you agreed with.

Ask your partner to tell you:

Two ways that you collaborated well in your group (write what they tell you here):

 ....

 ....

One way that you could improve your collaboration skills (write what they tell you here):

....

> **Independent reflection activity**
>
> **Check your learning goals**
> If you have achieved them and could teach someone else, put a '★'.
> If you have achieved them independently, put a '☺'.
> If you can achieve them with support, put a '☺'.

> **Self-assessment Lessons 1–2**
>
> **How will I know if I have achieved my learning goals?**
> Use this activity to reflect on how well you have progressed over the last two lessons.
> Tick (✓) 'Achieved independently' if you feel confident that you could apply this skill for yourself.
> Tick (✓) 'Achieved with support' if you still need some help when you apply this skill.

Continued

If you tick 'Achieved independently', then try to deepen your understanding and provide support for others when working on the next issue.

If you tick 'Achieved with support', look out for opportunities to consolidate this skill when working on the next issue.

Collaboration learning goals To start to:	Achieved independently	Achieved with support	I think this because
contribute useful ideas in my team			
help my team to solve problems			
help my team to plan tasks			
respect other team members' ideas about how to reach a goal			

Issue review

Think about the issue you have been focusing on and complete the following statements.

I was surprised to discover/explore that ....

....

I did not know ....

....

I now think ....

....

Developing collaboration skills: Lesson 3

Lesson learning goals		
These are the goals for this lesson. You will return to this table at the end of the lesson for the independent reflection activity.		
My learning goals **To develop my knowledge and understanding about:**	I think	My teacher/ partner thinks
working well with others to solve a problem		
working effectively in my team to plan a project		

What can I already do?

Arun and Zara's class are doing a science experiment. Read Arun and Zara's speech and then hold a class discussion to answer the questions below.

1 What do you think the problem was?
2 What was the outcome?
3 What was Zara and Arun's task?
4 Who helped her?
5 What can Zara and Arun feel proud about?
6 When have you worked with someone to achieve something that you felt proud of?
7 Who helped you?
8 What did you do?
9 What was the outcome?

> We were the class science monitors. We tried to make sure all of the equipment was given out properly.

> Each group had what they needed for the experiment, some groups had different results.

Starter activity

Can you complete the eight flowcharts? The first one has been done for you.

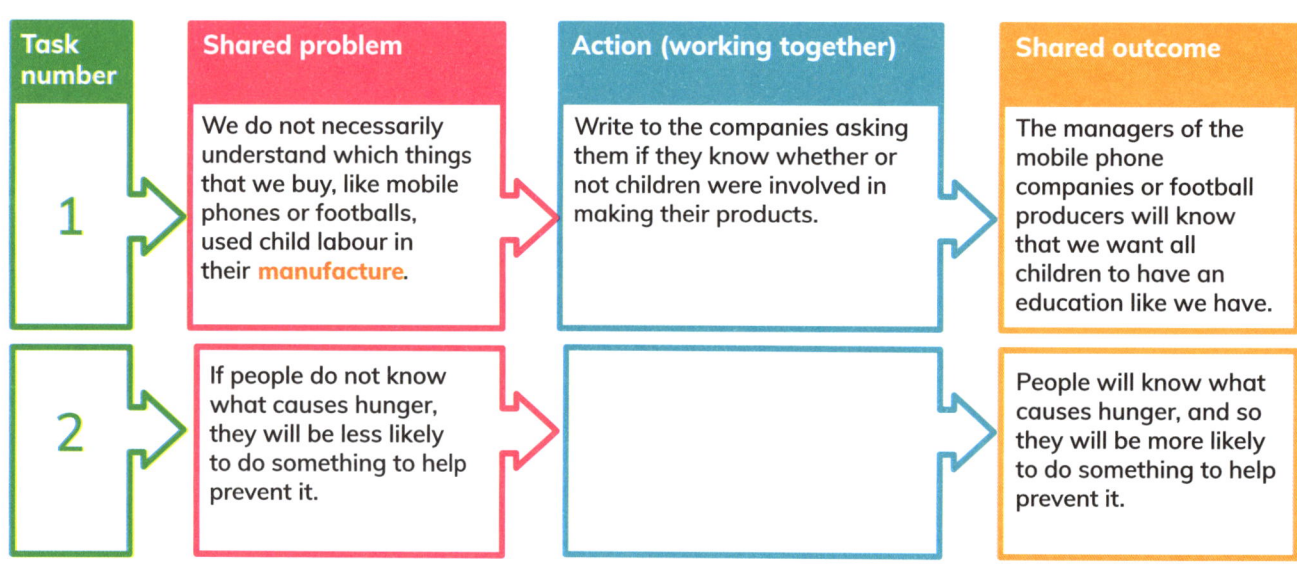

Task number	Shared problem	Action (working together)	Shared outcome
1	We do not necessarily understand which things that we buy, like mobile phones or footballs, used child labour in their **manufacture**.	Write to the companies asking them if they know whether or not children were involved in making their products.	The managers of the mobile phone companies or football producers will know that we want all children to have an education like we have.
2	If people do not know what causes hunger, they will be less likely to do something to help prevent it.		People will know what causes hunger, and so they will be more likely to do something to help prevent it.

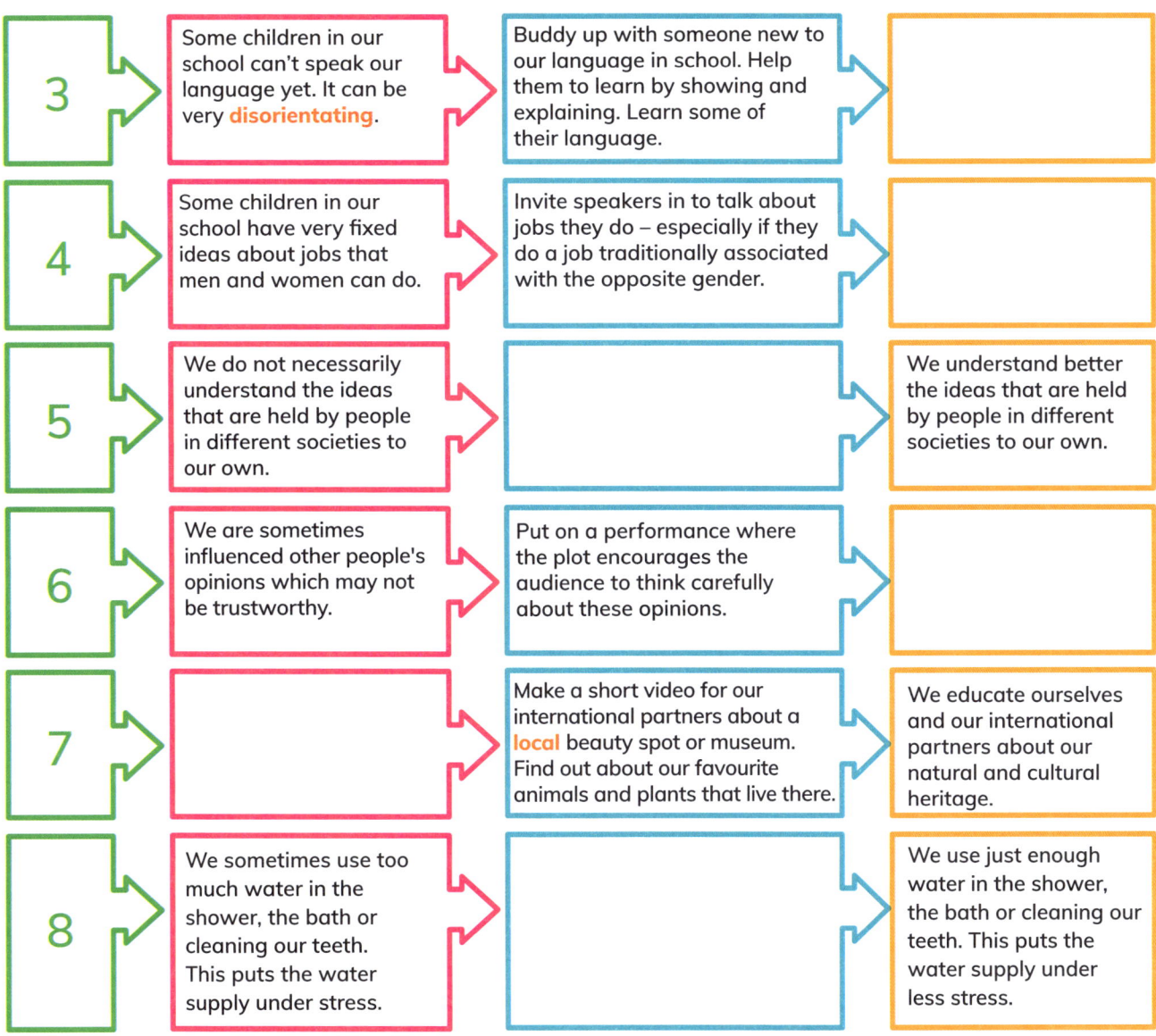

3	Some children in our school can't speak our language yet. It can be very **disorientating**.	Buddy up with someone new to our language in school. Help them to learn by showing and explaining. Learn some of their language.	
4	Some children in our school have very fixed ideas about jobs that men and women can do.	Invite speakers in to talk about jobs they do – especially if they do a job traditionally associated with the opposite gender.	
5	We do not necessarily understand the ideas that are held by people in different societies to our own.		We understand better the ideas that are held by people in different societies to our own.
6	We are sometimes influenced other people's opinions which may not be trustworthy.	Put on a performance where the plot encourages the audience to think carefully about these opinions.	
7		Make a short video for our international partners about a **local** beauty spot or museum. Find out about our favourite animals and plants that live there.	We educate ourselves and our international partners about our natural and cultural heritage.
8	We sometimes use too much water in the shower, the bath or cleaning our teeth. This puts the water supply under stress.		We use just enough water in the shower, the bath or cleaning our teeth. This puts the water supply under less stress.

Main activity

The issue I am focusing on today is:

....

Now complete this flowchart related to your issue.

Step 1:   In your group, identify three shared problems associated with your issue.
Record your ideas in the left-hand column of the flowchart.

Step 2:   For each one, decide what the outcome should be.
Record your ideas in the right-hand column of the flowchart.

Step 3:   Decide what action you could take together to get to the outcome.
Record your ideas in the middle column of the flowchart.

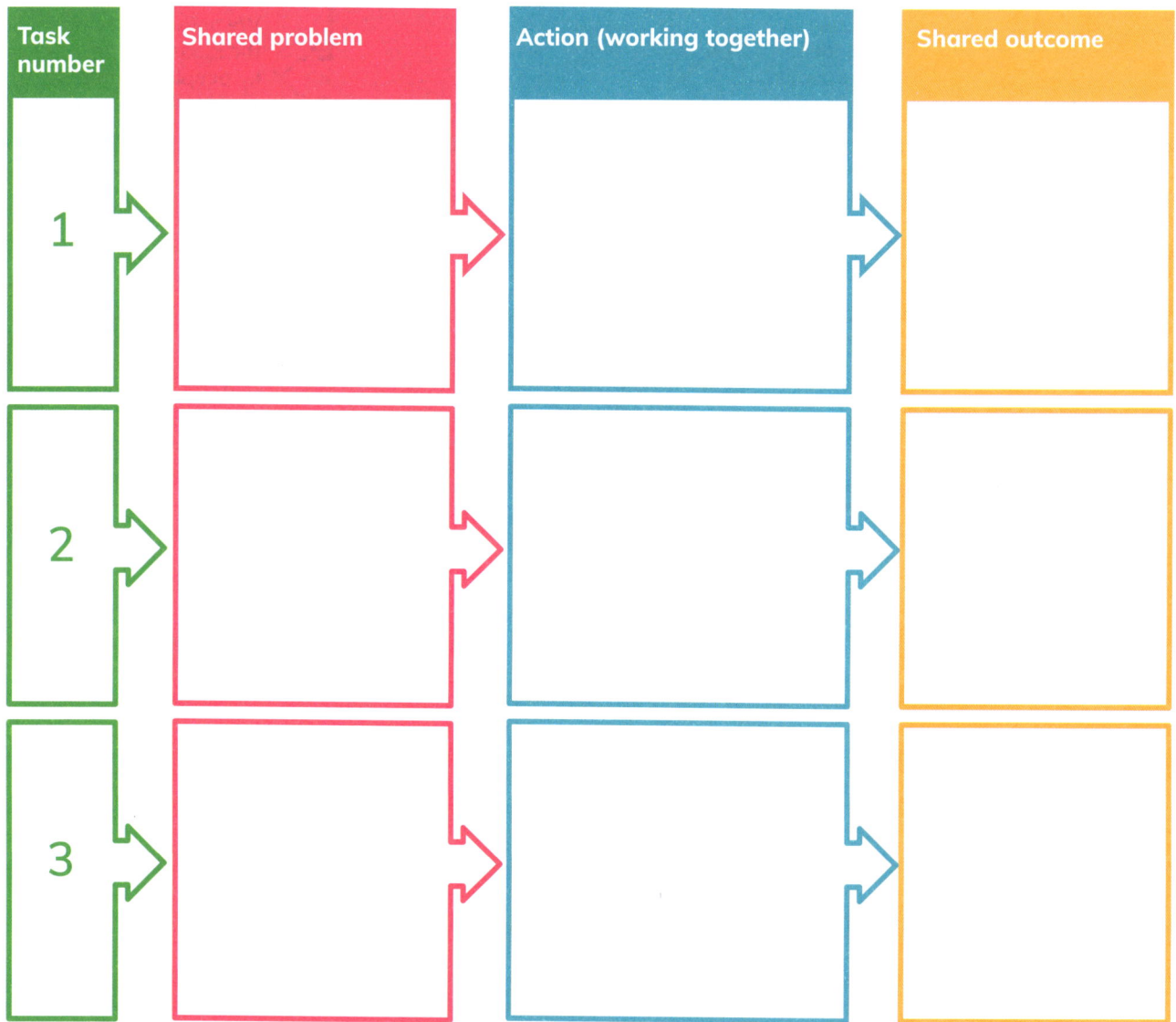

Task number	Shared problem	Action (working together)	Shared outcome
1			
2			
3			

Which action do you think you might go with, at this stage, if you only have time to take one action? You do not need to make a final decision right now, but here are some things to think about:

- Is it an important problem that needs action to be taken on?
- Will the action change the way people behave?
- Is the outcome realistic?
- Will you be able to work together as a team as part of your action?
- Will you need outside help – and is that help available?

The task that we are prioritising at this stage is ....

This is because, firstly, ...

In addition, ...

Furthermore, ...

Finally, ...

Be ready to report back to the class.

Class discussion

When listening to the other groups, be ready to offer constructive suggestions:

1   Have they identified an important problem that needs action to be taken on?
2   In what way(s) could their action change the way people behave?
    How could they improve?
3   Is the outcome realistic? Can they measure their success?
4   Will they be able to work together as a team as part of their action?
    Have they identified how they might divide this up?
5   Will they need outside help – and is that help available? Have you got any
    suggestions for who they could approach? Or could they do it all by themselves?

Share your ideas with others in the class.

Independent reflection activity

Check your learning goals

If you have achieved them and could teach someone else, put a '★'.

If you have achieved them independently, put a '☺'.

If you can achieve them with support, put a '☺'.

Developing collaboration skills: Lesson 4

Lesson learning goals		
These are the goals for this lesson. You will return to this table at the end of the lesson for the independent reflection activity.		

My learning goals To develop my knowledge and understanding about:	I think	My teacher/ partner thinks
working well with my team to overcome a challenge		
working effectively in my team to plan a project		

What can I already do?

Your goal is to work as a team to get each of your team members from the start line to the finish line. You will be given two skateboards, one piece of rope and a hockey stick for each team. No member of the team should put either their feet or hands on the floor during the task. The two skateboards, the piece of rope and the hockey stick must also cross the finish line. Based on what you know already about practical tasks and working in groups, what do you think is the best way that your group can do this?

Make a plan to break down the task into steps and decide what each member of the group is doing. You may find diagrams useful.

Starter activity

Complete the activity following the instructions that your teacher will give you.

Then reflect: How was the activity for you? Complete these sentences.

1 At first, I thought that ....would be a good idea.

2 I later found out that ....

3 A skill I brought to the group was ....

4 One good thing about working in a group was that ....

5 One difficulty of working in a group was ....

6 One way I could have improved my contribution to the group would have been to

   ....

7 If I did the activity again, I would ....

Main activity

The issue I am focusing on today is:

....

Last year, Marcus and Sofia were involved in an assembly to mark the 12 June United Nations Day of Action against child labour. This year, they have been in touch with their international partners and found out that many children there are forced to work in other people's homes to support their families.

They have decided to take action again and organised their ideas into a table.

The outcome we want is children being aware that other children have a right to an education too.

Our suggested actions are:

What? (suggest action)	When?	Where?	Who?	Why?
Give out stickers	The day before 12 June Day of Action	Outside during break time	Our group giving them to Stage 1 and 2 children	To help the younger children understand the message – gives us a chance to talk to them
Put on a football match between two girls' teams Give out postcard – 'Formula for Progress – Educate both girls and boys!' postcards to spectators	Lunch time and after school in the week leading up to 12 June	School pitch	Children and parents who like football	To highlight the fact that girls are more likely to end up involved in child labour
Perform the song 'Take a Stand' by the French band Kids United New Generation Give out the manifesto and the red card to parents	In the assembly on 12 June	School hall	Our group performing to the school and giving out the material as the parents enter	It is dedicated to the UN International Year for the Elimination of Child Labour, 2021

Either: Come up with further actions that your group thinks could help Marcus and Sofia meet their goal.

Or: Come up with actions that you think could help your group meet your goal.

The outcome we want is ....

Our suggested actions are:

What? (suggest action)	When?	Where?	Who?	Why?

Peer feedback

Work with a partner to find out how you showed collaboration skills in this lesson.

Ask them to what extent, in their opinion:

- you worked positively with others
- you helped the team to reach agreement when team members had different ideas about what the team should do
- you encouraged others to join in
- you made positive suggestions
- you were open to other group members' ideas.

Ask them to tell you:

Two things you did well (write what they tell you here):

 ....

 ....

One thing that you could do better (write what they tell you here):

 ....

Independent reflection activity

Check your learning goals

If you have achieved them and could teach someone else, put a '★'.

If you have achieved them independently, put a '☺'.

If you can achieve them with support, put a '☹'.

Self-assessment Lessons 3–4

How will I know if I have achieved my learning goals?

Use this activity to reflect on how well you have progressed over the last two lessons.

Tick (✓) 'Achieved independently' if you feel confident that you could apply this skill for yourself.

Tick (✓) 'Achieved with support' if you still need some help when you apply this skill.

If you tick 'Achieved independently', then try to deepen your understanding and provide support for others when working on the next issue.

If you tick 'Achieved with support', look out for opportunities to consolidate this skill when working on the next issue.

Continued

Collaboration learning goals To develop my knowledge and understanding about:	Achieved independently	Achieved with support	I think this because
working well with others to solve a problem or overcome a challenge			
working effectively in my team to plan a project			

Issue review

Think about the issue you have been focusing on and complete the following statements.

I was surprised to discover/explore that ....

....

I did not know ....

....

I now think ....

....

5

Getting better at collaboration skills: Lesson 5

Lesson learning goals

These are the goals for this lesson.
You will return to this table at the end of the lesson for the independent reflection activity.

My learning goals To get better at:	I think	My teacher/ partner thinks
introducing useful ideas to my team that help to achieve a shared goal		
planning as a team to achieve a shared goal, by dividing tasks among team members appropriately		

What can I already do?

Arun has written down some of the things he thinks are important for successful teamwork:

a dividing up the work appropriately

b encouraging others to do their best

c meeting deadlines

d listening to others

e making useful suggestions

f knowing what skills we need

Which of these things do you think is the most important? Which are important, and which are less important, in your opinion? Write them in the boxes below:

Most important

Important

Least important

Talk with a partner. Did you both choose the same thing as the 'most important'? Explain your choice to your partner. What else do you think is important for successful teamwork?

Starter activity

The issue I am focusing on today is:

....

Sofia's team took action because they wanted to raise other children's awareness about Child Labour Day on 12 June. Afterwards, they wrote some personal reflections about how their action went. Read the personal reflections, and think about your answers to the questions for class discussion.

Marcus's personal reflection	Arun's personal reflection
We were going to put up posters a week before 12 June telling everyone it was Child Labour Day. I was responsible for designing the poster, because I wanted to develop my design skills. When I showed it to the other team members, they said they wanted me to make some changes, so I went back and did it again all by myself. It took me a long time, which meant that the posters didn't get put up until 11 June.	We'd all agreed to give out Child Labour Day stickers at breaktime on 11 June, but only two of us were able to do it because the others were on cleaning duty and had to stay in and tidy the classroom. Our job was made even more difficult because we didn't have enough stickers for everyone, and my partner and I couldn't agree which children we should give them to.

Sofia's personal reflection	Zara's personal reflection
My job was to design and print out the stickers, because I wanted to develop my computing skills. Unfortunately, our printer at home broke down when I started printing the stickers. I spent a couple of days trying to deal with this problem but I was unable to find a solution. When I arrived at the school on 11 June, I had to explain to the others that I had only printed about half the number of stickers we needed.	I was one of the team members giving out stickers during break time on 11 June. My partner kept asking 'Do you know when Child Labour Day is?' and only gave stickers to children who knew the answer. I thought this was unfair, because most of the children hadn't seen the posters about Child Labour Day. I found it quite hard to explain about child labour to the younger children because our group had not thought about what skills we would need to do this successfully.

Class discussion

1   What problems did the team experience when they carried out their action?
2   Why did these problems happen?

Main activity

Work in a group. Your goal is to make useful suggestions about how Sofia's team could improve the way they plan and prepare to carry out their course of action.

Choose three of the problems described by Sofia's team in their personal reflections. For each problem that you choose, decide what the best solution would be.

Problem	Solution
1	
2	
3	

Report back to the class about one of the problems your group chose and the solution that you have suggested.

Independent reflection activity

Check your learning goals

If you have achieved them and could teach someone else, put a '★'.

If you have achieved them independently, put a '☺'.

If you can achieve them with support, put a '☺'.

Self-assessment Lesson 5

How will I know if I have achieved my learning goals?

Use this activity to reflect on how well you have progressed over the last lesson.

Tick (✓) 'Achieved independently' if you feel confident that you could apply this skill for yourself.

Tick (✓) 'Achieved with support' if you still need some help when you apply this skill.

If you tick 'Achieved independently', then try to deepen your understanding and provide support for others when working on the next issue.

Continued

If you tick 'Achieved with support', look out for opportunities to consolidate this skill when working on the next issue.

Collaboration learning goals To get better at:	Achieved independently	Achieved with support	I think this because
introducing useful ideas to my team that help to achieve a shared goal			
planning to achieve a shared goal, by dividing tasks among team members appropriately			

Reflect on your responses in your self-assessment and identify one area for improvement.

One skill I want to get even better at is:

....

How I will improve:

....

Issue review

Think about the issue you have been focusing on and complete the following statements.

I was surprised to discover/explore that ....

....

I did not know ....

....

I now think ....

....

Communication

In this section of your Learner's Skills Book you'll be developing your communication skills while thinking about interesting issues.

But what does communication involve?

How can you present information in different ways? How can you make the information as clear as possible so it can be easily understood by others?

How can you organise information when you present it to others? How can you highlight the most important facts?

Where does the information you're presenting come from?

Is there anything in someone else's presentation that you don't understand or would like to know more about?

Let's start thinking about communication!

In Section 6: Communication, you might choose to focus on the Challenge 'What is the cost of my stuff?' and the topic 'Looking after planet Earth'.

If you take on this Challenge, you and your group will carry out research into the cost of resources, analyse your results and then present what you have learned to a wider audience. Here are some questions you might ask yourselves as you prepare to present your information to others…

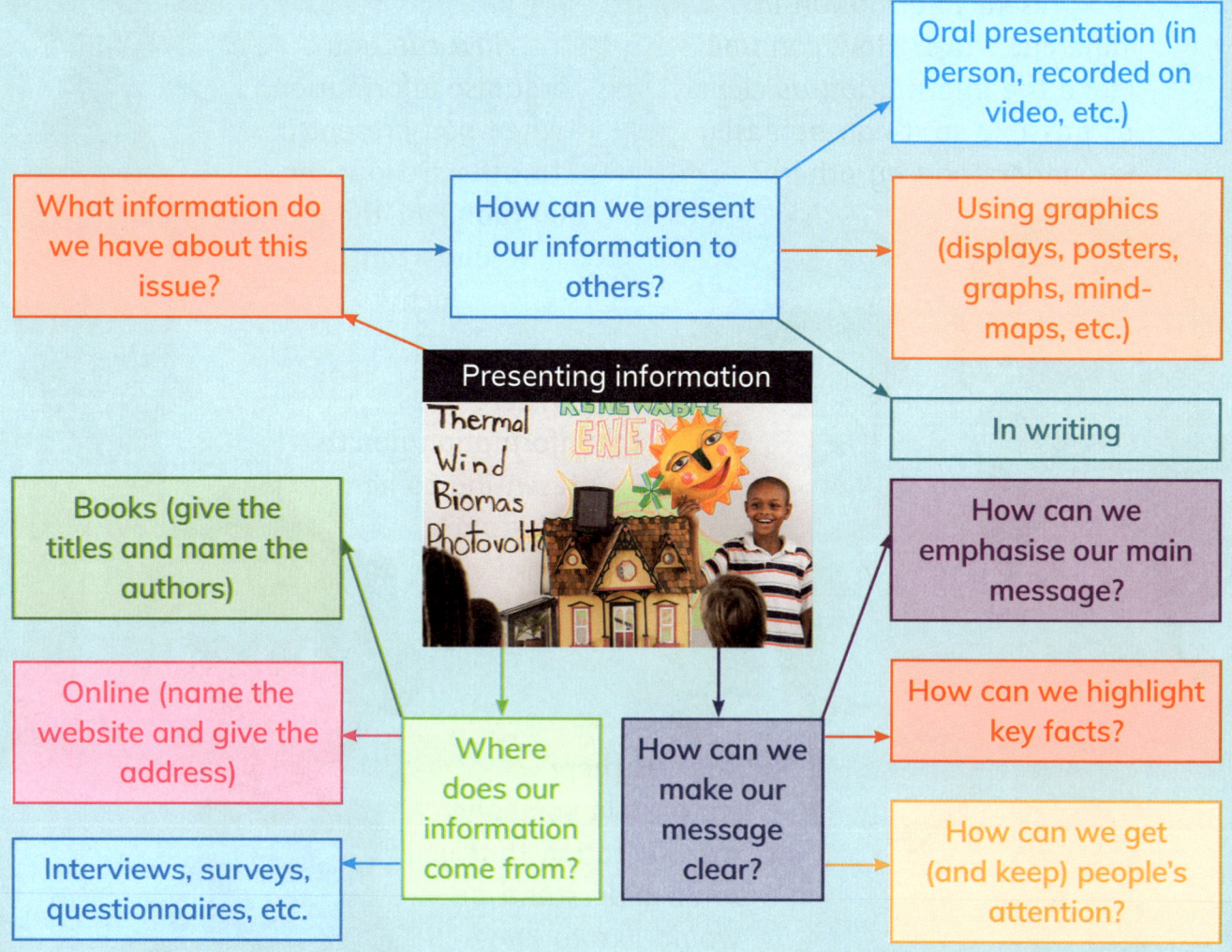

What information do we have about this issue?

How can we present our information to others?

Oral presentation (in person, recorded on video, etc.)

Using graphics (displays, posters, graphs, mind-maps, etc.)

In writing

Books (give the titles and name the authors)

Online (name the website and give the address)

Interviews, surveys, questionnaires, etc.

Where does our information come from?

How can we make our message clear?

How can we emphasise our main message?

How can we highlight key facts?

How can we get (and keep) people's attention?

Or you might choose to focus on the topics 'The world of work' and 'Education for all', which you will look at in this section of your Learner's Skills Book

Think about your answers to these questions:

- How can we help others to understand the information we're presenting?

- When I'm listening to others, what questions can I ask to make sure that I understand what they are saying?

Communication words

argument	information	persuasive	reasons	writing
debate	listening	presentation	speaking	
improvement	perspectives	reading	suggestion	

What is communication?

Communication: presenting information to others in ways that help them to understand it

Communication also includes:

- listening actively to others, and asking them questions to help you understand

Remember!

You can use any of the Challenges or topics as the starting point to develop your communication skills. Your teacher may direct you to focus on a specific Challenge or topic, or you may be able to choose for yourself.

Starting with communication skills: Lesson 1

In this chapter you will develop skills in **communication**. Communication means sending and responding to **information** by **speaking**, **writing** or using other media such as digital technologies. Communication also requires **skills** such as **listening** and **reading** so that information can be received.

Lesson learning goals		
These are the goals for this lesson. You will return to this table at the end of the lesson for the independent reflection activity.		
My learning goals **To start to:**	I think	My teacher/ partner thinks
tell other people about an issue so that they can understand it better		
listen to what someone tells me about an issue and respond by asking relevant questions		

What can I already do?

Sofia is taking part in a debate about how to improve her school. She has prepared a presentation with a clear structure setting out an argument about providing an area to encourage biodiversity.

Structure of my presentation

1) Introduction

2) Reasons to support my idea

3) Reasons to reject my idea

4) Conclusion

Using Sofia's numbers (1–4), give each part of her presentation a number to show where it fits in her structure. You will need to use some numbers more than once! An example has been done for you.

a   My name is Sofia, I'm a Year 5 student, and I'd like to propose that the school creates a biodiversity area. Why do I think this is important? Let me explain. **1**

b   As more and more of us live in cities, many children are losing touch with nature. Experts say that contact with nature improves young people's physical and mental health.

c   It can also give children more direct experience and knowledge of the natural world, instead of just reading about it in books or seeing it on screens.

d   Some people say that there isn't enough room in our school for a biodiversity area, and even if there was, it would be better to use it for extra classrooms.

e   However, classrooms are not the only places where children can learn – think of all the science experiments you could do in a biodiversity area!

f   So to give students the opportunity to learn more about nature by experiencing it for themselves, I urge the school to create a biodiversity area.

Talk with a partner and compare your work. Do you agree or disagree with Sofia?

Starter activity

The issue I am focusing on today is:

....

Zara and her group are discussing their ideas about what schools will be like in the future. Read their discussion.

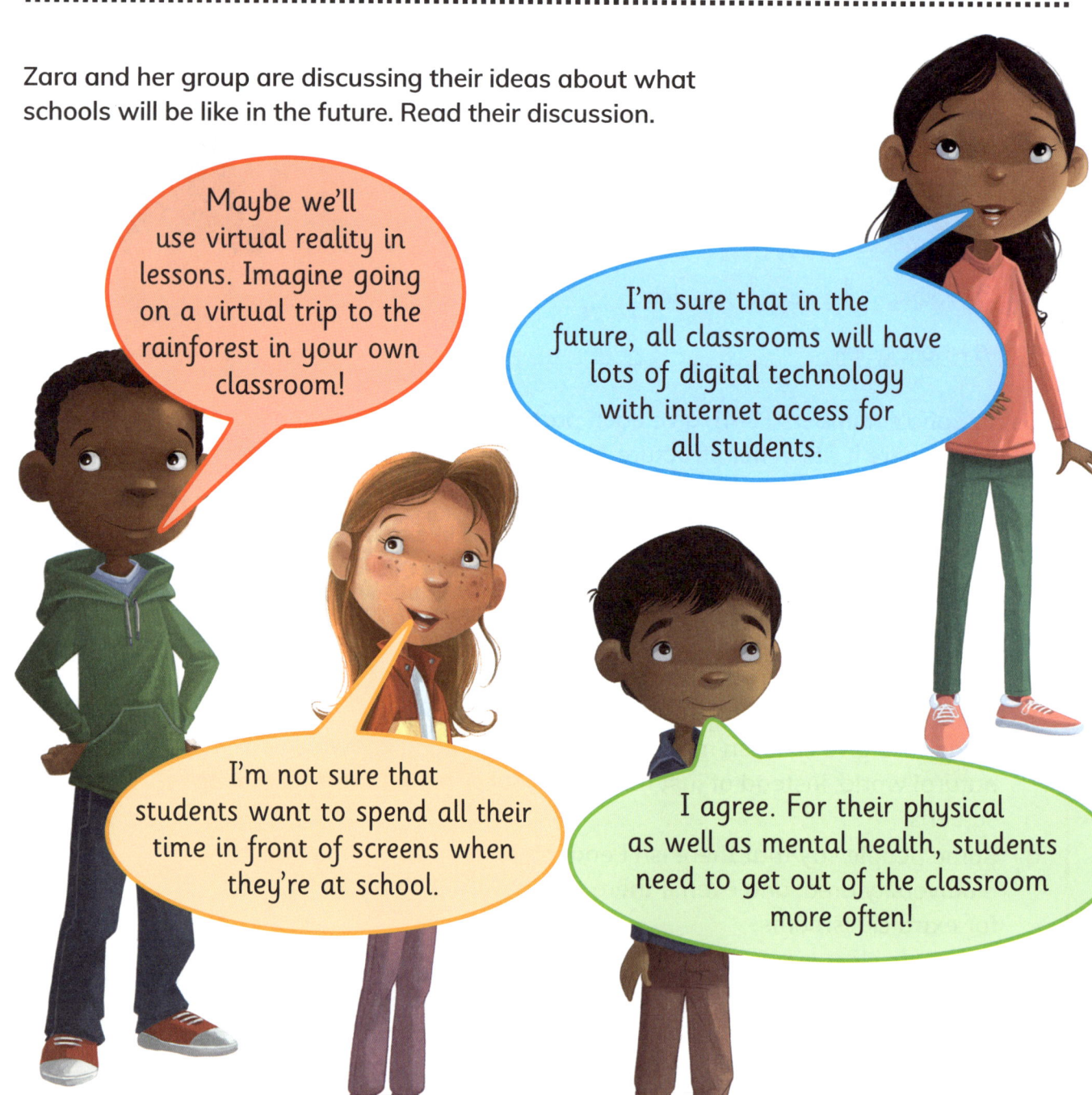

Maybe we'll use virtual reality in lessons. Imagine going on a virtual trip to the rainforest in your own classroom!

I'm sure that in the future, all classrooms will have lots of digital technology with internet access for all students.

I'm not sure that students want to spend all their time in front of screens when they're at school.

I agree. For their physical as well as mental health, students need to get out of the classroom more often!

Class discussion

1   In their discussion, Zara and Marcus look forward to using more technology in the classroom, while Sofia and Arun think that other ways of learning are important. Who do you agree with, and why?

2   Arun says that students 'need to get out of the classroom'.

    a   What things can students learn outside the classroom?

    b   What school activities do you do outside the classroom?

Main activity

Zara and her group look at the plan of a new school that is going to be built in their area. Your teacher will give you this in a download. Unfortunately, the plan is incomplete, because it doesn't show what each of the school buildings will be used for!

Work in a group. Your teacher will give each group member some information that will help you to complete the plan. Tell the other group members your information, and listen carefully to what the others tell you. Add labels to the plan to show what each of the buildings is.

Class discussion

1   What do you like about the school in the plan?

2   What do you think you would improve or change about the school in the plan? Ask questions to clarify other people's perspectives on why they think a change would be a good idea. Remember, a perspective is a viewpoint on an issue based on evidence and reasoning, so they should be able to explain their ideas.

Independent reflection activity

Check your learning goals

If you have achieved them and could teach someone else, put a '★'.

If you have achieved them independently, put a '☺'.

If you can achieve them with support, put a '☺'.

Starting with communication skills: Lesson 2

Lesson learning goals		
These are the goals for this lesson. You will return to this table at the end of the lesson for the independent reflection activity.		
My learning goals To start to:	I think	My teacher/ partner thinks
tell other people about an issue so that they can understand it better		
listen to what someone tells me about an issue and respond by asking relevant questions		

What can I already do?

Marcus is also taking part in a debate about how to improve his school, and he has prepared a presentation with a clear structure.

Structure of my presentation

1) Introduction

2) Reasons to support my idea

3) Reasons to reject my idea

4) Conclusion

Using Marcus's numbers (1–4), give each part of his presentation a number to show where it fits in his structure. You will need to use some numbers more than once! An example has been done for you.

a My name is Marcus, I'm a Year 5 student, and I'd like to propose an outdoor classroom for our school. I'll tell you why I think this is important, but first I'll explain what it is. `1`

b An outdoor classroom has a roof, but no walls, so that lessons are in the open air. There are benches to sit on, but no desks, creating plenty of space to move around in.

c Some people say that an outdoor classroom is a waste of money because you can't use it when the weather is bad, and students can't concentrate or don't take lessons seriously.

d However, experts say that spending more time in the open air is good for children's physical and mental development, and that fresh air can actually improve their concentration.

e In an outdoor classroom, students can move around more and create noise without disturbing others. Some children learn better like this than sitting all day in a traditional classroom.

f To conclude, students might only spend a few minutes a day in the outdoor classroom, but if it improves their health, their concentration and their learning, it would be worth it.

Talk with a partner and compare your work. Do you agree or disagree with Marcus?

Starter activity

The issue I am focusing on today is:

....

Zara's group are discussing ways to improve their school. Read their discussion, and then think about your answers to the questions for class discussion.

> I wish we had more places to play sport, such as a basketball court or a 5-a-side football pitch.

> I'd like our school to have a study centre where there are laptops or tablets with internet access for everyone.

> At my cousin's school, they've got an adventure playground that the children can play in at break time.

> If there was a music studio, I could learn to play the drums without disturbing our next-door neighbours!

Class discussion

1 Which of the **suggestions** that the group make do you prefer and why?
2 What are some of the reasons for or against their suggestions?

Main activity

Working on your own to begin with, think of something that could improve your school. Then think of some reasons to support your suggestion. (Can you also think of some reasons that might be used against your suggestion?) Make some notes and drawings to help you explain your idea.

Now work in a group. Your group's goal is to choose one **improvement** that could be made to your school and decide the reasons you could use to support your idea.

Tell the others in the group your suggestion and your reasons to support it. Listen to everyone else's suggestions, and ask questions if there's anything you want to know, or if something isn't clear to you.

Your group should choose one suggestion to focus on. Write it here, and note down the argument you will use to support it:

Our group's suggestion: ....

....

....

....

Our argument to support it:

....

....

....

....

....

Peer feedback

Talk to a partner from a different group. Tell your partner your group's suggestion and the argument to support it. Then listen to your partner tell you about their group's suggestion, and ask some questions about it.

When you've done this, ask your partner to answer YES or NO to these statements:

I presented my group's suggestion in a clear way.   Yes/No

I listened carefully to my partner's suggestion.   Yes/No

I asked my partner some questions.   Yes/No

If the answer is 'NO', ask your partner what improvements you could make.

Independent reflection activity

Check your learning goals

If you have achieved them and could teach someone else, put a '★'.

If you have achieved them independently, put a '☺'.

If you can achieve them with support, put a '☹'.

Self-assessment Lessons 1–2

How will I know if I have achieved my learning goals?

Use this activity to reflect on how well you have progressed over the last two lessons.

Tick (✓) 'Achieved independently' if you feel confident that you could apply this skill for yourself.

Tick (✓) 'Achieved with support' if you still need some help when you apply this skill.

If you tick 'Achieved independently', then try to deepen your understanding and provide support for others when working on the next issue.

If you tick 'Achieved with support', look out for opportunities to consolidate this skill when working on the next issue.

Continued

Communication learning goals To start to:	Achieved independently	Achieved with support	I think this because
tell other people about an issue so that they can understand it better			
listen to what someone tells me about an issue and respond by asking relevant questions			

Issue review

Think about the issue you have been focusing on and complete the following statements.

I was surprised to discover/explore that ....

....

I did not know ....

....

I now think ....

....

Developing communication skills: Lesson 3

Lesson learning goals		
These are the goals for this lesson. You will return to this table at the end of the lesson for the independent reflection activity.		
My learning goals To develop my knowledge and understanding about:	I think	My teacher/ partner thinks
presenting information on an issue using a clear structure		
referring to sources that I have used		

What can I already do?

Arun is also taking part in the debate. He has not always presented information clearly, so some of the people who have listened to his presentation ask questions to try to understand better. Match each of the questions to the relevant part of Arun's presentation. One example has been done for you.

1 What are the negative effects of spending too long doing this?

2 What exactly are you proposing?

3 What do you mean by 'new technology'?

4 When you say 'traditional ways of learning', what do you mean by that?

5 Why do students need to be in contact with each other outside school?

a My name is Arun, and I'm a Year 5 student. I'd like to explain why every student at our school would benefit from my proposal. **[1]**

b We're living in a world where understanding new technology is really important, and everyone needs to learn how to use it.

c A **UNICEF** report about **remote learning** shows that technology including mobile phones can really help children, families and teachers work together.

d Some people say that young people spend too much time sitting in front of screens, and this can be harmful to them.

e However, the new technology is our future, and traditional ways of learning have to change. School should help us prepare for future success!

Talk with a partner and compare your work.
What do you think are the answers to the questions?

Starter activity

The issue I am focusing on today is:

....

Zara's group have chosen Sofia's suggestion that their school should have an adventure playground. They plan to give a group presentation, putting forward their proposal to the rest of the class. Read their plan, and then think about the questions for class discussion.

Adventure playground presentation

PLAN

Introduction - Sofia
Our group's proposal = adventure playground
Explain what it is

Reasons for (1) - Arun
Children will be more active at break-times
Westside Observer article shows the positive impact on health and wellbeing

Reasons against - Zara
Dangerous? Children might injure themselves
Not educational?

Reasons for (2) / Response to reasons against - Marcus
Children learn to play safely, develop social skills by helping each other
Adults must supervise at all times

Conclusion - Sofia
Repeat reasons for
Good way to improve school - keeps children healthy and happy!
Ask for questions from the audience

Class discussion

1   Why do you think the group have structured their presentation in this way?

2   Which member of the group made it clear where they got their information from?

3   Do you think they should write down exactly what each person is going to say? Give reasons for your answer.

4   What could Zara's group do to keep their audience's attention during their presentation?

Main activity

Look at the group decision you made in Lesson 2 and make a plan of how your group will present your proposal. Decide who will give each part of the presentation and what each person will talk about. Make sure that you include in your plan where you got your information from. You can use the same structure for your presentation as Zara's group, or create your own structure.

Remember to rehearse your presentation as a group to make sure that your plan works!

Independent reflection activity

Check your learning goals

If you have achieved them and could teach someone else, put a '★'.

If you have achieved them independently, put a '☺'.

If you can achieve them with support, put a '☺'.

Developing communication skills: Lesson 4

Lesson learning goals		
These are the goals for this lesson. You will return to this table at the end of the lesson for the independent reflection activity.		
My learning goals To develop my knowledge and understanding about:	I think	My teacher/ partner thinks
presenting information on an issue using a clear structure		
listening to ideas and information about an issue, and asking relevant questions		

What can I already do?

Zara's group are preparing to give a group presentation. Which of the following do you think is the most important for giving a successful presentation? Which are important and which are less important? Write them in the boxes below.

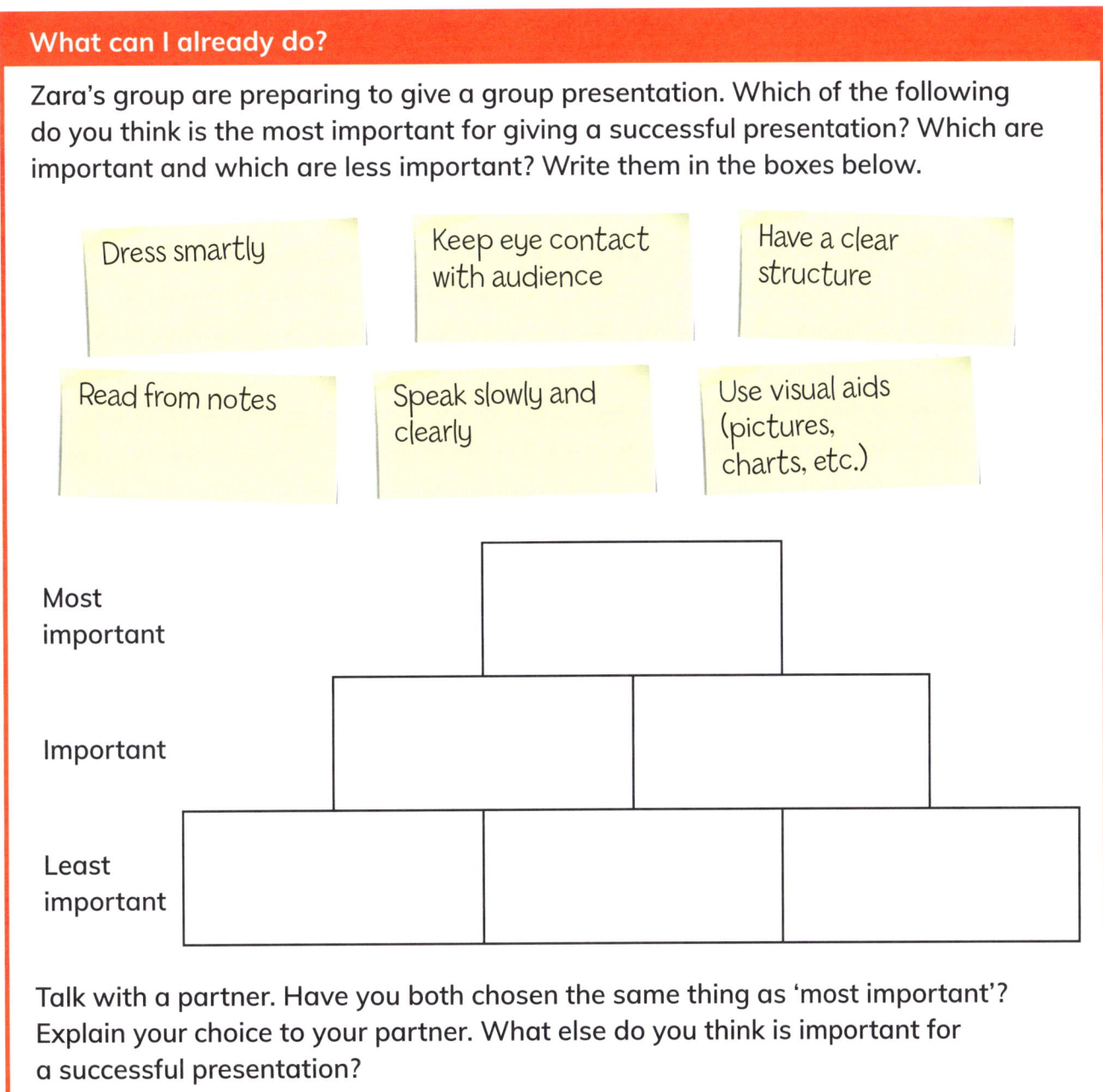

Dress smartly

Keep eye contact with audience

Have a clear structure

Read from notes

Speak slowly and clearly

Use visual aids (pictures, charts, etc.)

Most important

Important

Least important

Talk with a partner. Have you both chosen the same thing as 'most important'? Explain your choice to your partner. What else do you think is important for a successful presentation?

Starter activity

Zara's group gave their presentation about adventure playgrounds to their class (see their plan in Lesson 3). Afterwards, each of the group members reflected on how well the presentation went. Read what they have written in their personal reflections, and think about your answers to the questions for class discussion.

Sofia's reflection	Arun's reflection
Overall, I think that our presentation went well. Most of us spoke clearly, and our presentation had a clear structure. However, I don't think the audience really understood what an adventure playground is. I tried to explain it to them in my introduction, but I could also have held up some pictures to show them what it looks like.	When it was my turn to speak, I panicked a bit, and forgot some of the things I wanted to say. However, the others in the group helped me, so I was able to include all my reasons for having an adventure playground. Next time, I think I'll write down some notes to remind me what to say.

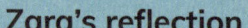

Zara's reflection	Marcus' reflection
I'm not used to speaking in front of an audience, so I wrote down everything I wanted to say on some cards. That made me feel more confident, but when it was my turn, I started to speak too quickly. Then someone in the audience stopped me to ask a question because they couldn't understand what I was saying! It really confused me!	I spoke my part well, and kept eye contact with the audience while I was speaking, so I could see that they understood me. The audience asked some good questions at the end, which showed that they'd listened carefully. So we succeeded in keeping their attention, but I'm not sure if they agreed with our proposal.

Class discussion

1 What went well in the presentation, according to the group members?
2 What could be changed or improved next time?

Main activity

The issue I am focusing on today is:

....

Look at the plan that your group made in Lesson 3 for a group presentation about how to improve your school. Your group is going to give your presentation to an audience, but there will be a strict time limit of 5 minutes for each group. Check your plan, and see if you need to make any changes or prepare anything before you give your presentation. Good luck!

As you listen to other groups giving their presentations, remember to ask questions if there's anything that you don't understand or that you'd like to know more about.

Peer feedback

Work with a partner who has listened to your group's presentation.
Ask them to tell you: Two things that they liked about the presentation
your group gave (write what they tell you here):

★ ....
★ ....

One thing that you could do better (write what they tell you here):

 ....

Independent reflection activity

Check your learning goals

If you have achieved them and could teach someone else, put a '★'.

If you have achieved them independently, put a '☺'.

If you can achieve them with support, put a '☺'.

Self-assessment Lessons 3–4

How will I know if I have achieved my learning goals?

Use this activity to reflect on how well you have progressed over the last two lessons.

Tick (✓) 'Achieved independently' if you feel confident that you could apply this skill for yourself.

Tick (✓) 'Achieved with support' if you still need some help when you apply this skill.

If you tick 'Achieved independently', then try to deepen your understanding and provide support for others when working on the next issue.

If you tick 'Achieved with support', look out for opportunities to consolidate this skill when working on the next issue.

Communication learning goals To develop my knowledge and understanding about:	Achieved independently	Achieved with support	I think this because
presenting information on an issue using a clear structure			
referring to sources that I have used			
listening to ideas and information about an issue and asking relevant questions			

Issue review

Think about the issue you have been focusing on and complete the following statements.

I was surprised to discover/explore that ....

....

I did not know ....

....

I now think ....

....

Getting better at communication skills: Lesson 5

Lesson learning goals		
These are the goals for this lesson. You will return to this table at the end of the lesson for the independent reflection activity.		
My learning goals To get better at:	I think	My teacher/ partner thinks
presenting information on an issue using a clear structure, referring to sources I have used		
listening to ideas and information about an issue and responding by asking relevant questions		

What can I already do?

Imagine someone told you that they had a way to build new schools using a prefabricated system. They say their schools are low cost and easy to build. They also say that children who live in remote areas or other areas with no schools can benefit.

What questions would you ask them?

Share your ideas in a class discussion.

Starter activity

Sofia has been listening carefully to Marcus's discussion of the benefits of outdoor learning. She has annotated a transcript of Marcus's speech – your teacher will give you this in a download.

In your pairs, one person should take the role of Marcus; the other should take the role of Sofia.

1   How do you think Marcus would respond to Sofia's questions?
2   How do you think Sofia would respond to Marcus's answers?

Main activity

The issue I am focusing on today is:

....

Work with a partner.

1   Listen carefully as they tell you their plan for how to improve your school.
    They will give you a transcript of what they say.
2   Follow their speech by reading the transcript as they present their ideas.
    Annotate their transcript the way Sofia did with Marcus's speech.
3   Ask your partner questions.
4   Listen carefully to their answers.
5   If you need to, ask further questions for clarification.

Class discussion

What idea did you think was the most persuasive?

Independent reflection activity

Check your learning goals

If you have achieved them and could teach someone else, put a '★'.

If you have achieved them independently, put a '☺'.

If you can achieve them with support, put a '☺'.

Self-assessment Lesson 5

How will I know if I have achieved my learning goals?

Use this activity to reflect on how well you have progressed over the last lesson.

Tick (✓) 'Achieved independently' if you feel confident that you could apply this skill for yourself.

Tick (✓) 'Achieved with support' if you still need some help when you apply this skill.

If you tick 'Achieved independently', then try to deepen your understanding and provide support for others when working on the next issue.

If you tick 'Achieved with support', look out for opportunities to consolidate this skill when working on the next issue.

Communication learning goals To get better at:	Achieved independently	Achieved with support	I think this because
presenting information on an issue using a clear structure, referring to sources I have used			

Continued

Communication learning goals To get better at:	Achieved independently	Achieved with support	I think this because
listening to ideas and information about an issue and responding by asking relevant questions			

Reflect on your responses in your self-assessment and identify one area for improvement.

One skill I want to get even better at is:

....

How I will improve:

....

Issue review

Think about the issue you have been focusing on and complete the following statements.

I was surprised to discover/explore that ....

....

I did not know ....

....

I now think ....

....

Glossary

agreement	when more than one person shares the same opinion or perspective on an issue or topic. This may happen when people share their own perspective, or may be something that happens as people start to discuss their views and someone is persuaded to share another person's opinion.
analysis	in general, looking at something in more detail, for example, in order to understand the different parts that it consists of. In Cambridge Primary Global Perspectives, analysis may involve understanding different perspectives on a topic or issue, or how different causes and consequences are related to one another. Analysis may also involve understanding data presented as numbers or in the form of graphs, charts or tables.
answer	a response to a question that may be the aim of your research when researching an issue.
antivirus software	a programme designed to protect a computer against harmful codes designed to change the way it works.
argument	a series of statements containing reasons and evidence which support a claim about a local or global issue.
attributes	attitudes and life skills.
author	a person who writes something. They could be the creator of a book, an article or written content on a website.
bandwidth	the rate at which data can be transferred.
behaviour	the way that someone acts. This could be good or bad and your teacher may reward for good behaviour.
benefits	good points that may come out of a task, or working together as part of a team. These may also include good points about a certain perspective.
biodiversity	different kinds of plant and animal life. This could be in the world or in a particular place. Scientists consider that a high level of biodiversity is a good thing.

blog	a website or web page. It is updated regularly. Often it is created by a single writer. The style is usually informal.
browsing	scanning the internet.
campaigner	someone who organises or takes part in activities to try to achieve something.
carbon footprint	the amount of carbon dioxide that is released as the result of a process or activity.
categorise	to divide people or things into groups of similar types.
cause	the reason why something happens. For example, one of the causes of global warming is the burning of fossil fuels.
challenges	problems that we may face and need to work either individually or as a group to try and fix. These problems may be the result of an action.
chart	a type of picture that helps to explain data and/or numbers. In maths and computing, we use different types of charts to explain data.
child labour	work done by children that isn't appropriate for them, deprives children of their childhood and interferes with their ability to go to school.
click bait	online material designed to attract attention and tempt internet users to click on a link to a web page.
climate change	the way the Earth's weather is changing.
collaboration	working together with other people to achieve a shared outcome or to resolve an issue or problem.
communication	sending and responding to information by speaking, writing or using other media such as digital technologies. Communication also requires skills such as listening and reading so that information can be received.
company	an organisation that sells goods or services.
compromise	an agreement that usually means that both sides make some changes in order to settle a disagreement.
conference	an event at which people hold formal discussions about a topic. An example would be a peace conference to try and end a conflict between two or more nations.
confident	positive about your ability to do things well.

cons	the drawbacks or bad points that may come out of doing a task, a perspective or working as part of a team. You might look at the pros and cons, weighing both up, before deciding on doing a task.
consequence	the result of something. For example, global warming is the consequence of burning fossil fuels such as coal, natural gas and oil.
consolidate	to pull together and strengthen, e.g. your knowledge and understanding.
contribution	what a person offers to a project, in terms of their skills or actions. Within a team, this may be the skills or previous experience that someone can offer.
convenience	when something is easy to use and suitable for what you want to do.
cookies	data that help the owners of a website know who is accessing it.
data	information, especially numbers or facts.
deadline	a time by which something must be done.
debate	often spoken and can involve a presentation by speakers who will have different opinions on an issue. A type of formal disagreement where speakers may try to persuade others to share their opinion.
derelict	a derelict building or piece of land is not used any more and is in a bad condition.
disagreement	when people do not share the same opinion on a matter.
discrimination	unfair treatment of someone because of their sex, race, religion, etc.
disorientating	if someone is disorientated, they do not know where to go or what to do.
distraught	extremely upset and unhappy
effectively	in a way that is successful and achieves what you want.
encouraged	to support someone to do something.
environmental campaigner	someone who tries to raise people's awareness of threats to the environment such as pollution or climate change, and encourages people to make changes to prevent these threats.

evaluate	to consider or study something carefully and decide how good or bad it is.
evaluation	in general, deciding if something is useful for a particular purpose. In Cambridge Primary Global Perspectives, evaluation may involve deciding how useful a source of information is, or how effective an argument for or against something is, etc.
evidence	information about a global issue that helps to develop understanding or prove that something is true or false.
exports	products that are sold in a different country from the place they were made.
fact	something that you know is true, can be checked, exists or has happened.
findings	the results of your research and what you have found out.
fossil fuels	fuels, such as gas, coal and oil, that were formed underground from plant and animal remains millions of years ago.
global	anything that relates to the whole world. For example, a global perspective is a perspective on an issue that has impacts right across planet Earth.
graph	a type of picture that helps to explain data . In maths and computing, we use different types of graphs to explain data.
greenhouse gases	gases such as carbon dioxide and methane that cause the atmosphere to warm up.
grumpily	adverb describing someone's actions who is easily annoyed and often complaining.
improvement	to make something better than it was before, through an action or change that is introduced.
in-depth	to study something in lots of detail. This may involve research into an issue to understand it more fully.
infer	to work out that something is true because of the information that you have.
information	facts about a situation, person, event, etc.
innovative/ innovativeness	thinking up new methods or ideas.

International Labour Organization	the International Labour Organization (ILO) is part of the United Nations. It promotes justice for working people.
internet safety	knowing how to protect yourself from harm when you are using digital devices that are connected to the internet.
interview	a type of research where you ask someone questions that you have already prepared. You will note down their answers to your questions as part of your research to find out more information about something.
investigation	studying or researching an issue or topic when you want to find out more about something. You might look at different sources to gather facts and figures to help you understand more about the topic.
irrigation systems	ways to provide water for an area of land so that crops can be grown.
issue	an important subject or problem for discussion. People will have different perspectives on issues.
jpeg	a digital image format that includes a way of compressing digital images so that they can be easily transferred.
landfill	the process of getting rid of large amounts of rubbish by burying it, or a place where rubbish is buried.
learning goals	points that you want to understand and achieve by the end of a lesson.
limitations	if you describe something (for example a source) as having limitations you mean that it may be good for some things but it is not good for others.
listening	using your ears to hear what is being said and understand what you are being told. You may hear information, which you then need to understand in terms of how this helps your research.
local	anything that relates to a particular area. For example, a local perspective is a perspective on the impact of an issue in a relatively small area, such as a town or city.
local government	the control and organisation of towns and small areas, and the services they provide, by people who are elected by those living in the area.

logical	if an argument or perspective is logical it has one or more reasons why it should be supported.
manifesto	a published statement of a group's aims or intentions.
manipulate	to control someone or something in a clever way so that they do what you want them to do.
manufacture	to produce something, usually in large numbers in a factory.
method	the way that something is done. For example, in cooking the way that you are told to cook something in a recipe is a cooking method. In research, your research method will be how you decide to do your research. This could be questionnaires or interviews.
minister	a politician who is in charge of an important government department, such as agriculture, industry, transport, education, etc.
national	anything that relates to a particular country. For example, a national perspective is a perspective on an issue that has impacts right across that country.
negotiations	discussions in order to reach a deal or an agreement.
nitrogen dioxide	a poisonous brown gas that is formed when some metals dissolve.
notes	often written down and these are points that you want to come back to later as part of your research. You might take notes when you are interviewing someone so that you have a way to record what someone has said in an interview.
opinion	a view or a judgement that you form in your own mind about an issue.
overwhelm	if a feeling or situation overwhelms someone, it has an effect that is too strong or extreme.
particulate	an extremely small piece of dirt, especially one produced by road vehicles, that causes pollution.
personal	anything that relates to you as an individual. For example, your own individual way of looking at a topic is your personal perspective.
perspective	a viewpoint on an issue based on evidence and reasoning.
persuasive	able to make people agree to do something.

podcast	an audio file which can be downloaded to a computer or mobile device and listened to.
politician	someone who works in politics, sometimes a member of the government.
positive suggestions	good ideas that a team member may share with the team to help achieve a goal. In presentations, these may be points that people say to help you to improve your presentation skills.
possible	used when something is not certain.
potential	may develop into something (good or bad) in the future.
poverty	the state of being very poor.
prediction	a guess at what the outcome of research may be, based upon evidence.
prefabricated	referring to a building that has already been partly built when it is put together.
presentation	using either images or slides to deliver information to a group of people, and talking about what the images or slides show.
preventable	something that it is possible to stop from happening.
primary school	schools for children who are usually between the ages of 5 and 11; in some parts of the world, these are also called elementary or junior schools.
problem	a situation that causes difficulties and that needs to be dealt with.
profit	money that you get from selling goods or services for more than they cost to produce or provide.
progress	part of learning and is a way for you to see how much you have learnt about something along the way. This acts as a way for you to see how your skills have improved between now and when you started.
props	objects that are used in a film or a play (short for 'properties').
pros	the benefits or good points that may come out of doing a task, a perspective or working as part of a team. You might look at the pros and cons, weighing both up, before deciding on doing a task.
psychiatrist	a professional in psychiatry; psychiatry is the study and treatment of mental illness.

purpose	the aim of something. In research, this could be the aim of your research. When looking at a source, this means trying to work out what the author's aim was for writing this source and how their aim reflects their perspective.
question	a point that you ask people, as part of research, to find out more about a topic. You might ask questions as part of an interview or a questionnaire.
questionnaire	a form that contains questions. You might use this as part of research and ask people to fill this in so that you can look at the results from lots of people and understand what people think about a certain topic or issue.
ransomware	a type of software designed by criminals. It will stop a user from using their computer until money is paid.
reading	a type of skill where you can understand written information. You may use this skill as part of research to understand information from written sources.
reason	a fact about why something happens or why someone does something. Also means the ability to think about and make good decisions.
record	to note down results or findings that have come from your research. For example, if you were interviewing people about the type of journeys they have made you would need to note down what they say to look back on these answers later.
reflection	in general, thinking about or considering something in depth. In Cambridge Primary Global Perspectives, reflection may involve thinking about how well you have achieved your learning goals, how your thinking about an issue or your behaviour has changed, how much progress you have made in developing your skills, etc. You may also be expected to reflect on your personal contribution to a team effort, and on the benefits and challenges of working as a team.
reflective	thinking carefully (especially about your own learning or understanding).
remote	far away.
remote learning	teaching and learning that happens online instead of in a classroom. In remote learning the teacher and the learner do not meet up in the same place.

research	in general, investigating an issue or topic in order to get information about it. In Cambridge Primary Global Perspectives, research may involve making questions or predictions to help you find out more about an issue, finding sources that contain useful information, carrying out investigations using interviews and/or questionnaires, and presenting the results of an investigation.
resilience	the ability to deal appropriately with setbacks and reach the best possible outcome.
resolution	coming to an agreement to try and fix problems.
resourcefulness	the ability to act on your own – especially when normal supplies are unavailable.
responsibility	the ability to take charge of something in a mature way.
responsible	having the duty to deal with someone or something.
role	within teamwork, this means the job that you as an individual will do and what actions you will take to help the team complete their goal.
sceptic	someone who doubts that a belief or an idea is true or useful.
shared drive	a shared place on a computer network where users can easily store, search and access files from any connected device.
shared outcome	when two or more people agree on a result. This could be agreeing on a perspective, or agreeing on the result of research. Within teamwork, this could mean a goal that all team members have been working towards.
significant	important or noticeable.
sketch	in this sense, a short written or spoken story. At other times, it can mean a type of drawing.
skills	things that you are good at and may have done before. In a team, your skills may mean that you are given a certain task as you know how to do that task best.
social media	forms of electronic communication that allow people to share information using the internet or mobile phones.
solution	an answer to a problem, or a way to fix a problem.
source	anything written, spoken or visual/graphic that gives you information about a topic.

speaking	a type of skill where you talk to others and share your opinion on an issue or topic. You will use speaking skills as part of communication and to work together with others as part of a team.
strengths	for a person, these are things that you are good at. As part of a perspective, these are points that are good about that perspective and where the speaker/author is confident about what they are saying. They may have evidence to back-up their beliefs.
submerge	to go under the surface of water.
subsidy	money given as part of the cost of something to help or encourage it to happen.
suggestion	an idea that you might share with your team members, when working as part of a team. This could be something that you say to help the team to achieve a goal or complete work.
survey	a type of form that contains questions for people to answer. You might use a survey as part of research to help gather people's opinions on a topic.
sustainability	the idea that people must treat the environment with care so that there will be enough resources left in the future.
sustainable	when you describe something as 'sustainable' it means that it helps people to meet their needs now but does not stop other people from meeting their own needs in the future.
symbol	a sign, shape or object which is used to show an idea. For example, a heart shape is a symbol of love.
table	a type of picture that helps to explain data. This will often have lines going up and down, like a grid, to help you understand the information. In maths and computing, we use different types of tables to explain data.
tableaux vivants	a tableau vivant is a 'living picture', using people to recreate a scene without moving, as if in a photograph. They are also known as 'freeze frames'.

teamwork	working together with other people to complete a task or project. This means dividing work up fairly so that team members have an equal share of the work involved. Work may be given to team members based on their skills or previous experience.
tech company	a business that works in the field of digital electronics, software or internet services.
terms and conditions	rules that users must agree to before they can use a service such as an app or a website.
topic	a subject that you talk, write or find out about.
treaty	a written agreement between two or more countries.
trustworthy	when looking at a source, you believe what the author says about a topic as you feel that their opinion is true and hasn't been affected by other factors. Opinions may be affected by the author's purpose for writing, their values or certain groups that they belong to.
UNICEF	abbreviation of United Nations Children's Emergency Fund: a part of the United Nations Organisation. They work across the world to improve children's health, safety and education.
United Nations (UN)	an international organisation that tries to solve world problems in a peaceful way.
unprecedented	never having happened before.
untrustworthy	when looking at a source, you do not believe what the author says about a topic as you feel that their opinion has been affected by other factors. Opinions may be affected by the author's purpose for writing, their values or certain groups that they belong to.
vibrant	full of excitement and energy.
Venn diagram	a diagram with overlapping circles for sorting items into two (or more) groups, while also allowing items to belong to more than one group by being placed in the overlapping section(s).
word cloud	a way of showing the importance or frequency of words connected with a topic. In a word cloud, the more important or more frequent a word is, the bigger it appears.
writing	putting your thoughts, ideas and opinions down on paper, usually using pen/pencil and paper. A type of communication skill to show that you have an understanding of a topic.